WARRIOR
MOTHER

WARRIOR MOTHER

》》 ■ 《《

Fierce Love,
Unbearable Loss,
and Rituals that Heal

Sheila K Collins, PhD

SHE WRITES PRESS

Published 2013
Printed in the United States of America
ISBN: 978-1-938314-46-9
Library of Congress Control Number: 2013933276

For information, address:
She Writes Press
1563 Solano Ave #546
Berkeley, CA 94707

To my grandchildren
Ethan John, William Collin, Vitoria Mae, and Kyra Joy
May the stories in this volume help you to know more fully the joy you
have brought to your family and ensure you will never forget how much
you are loved.

CONTENTS

Preface. 1

Part One

Coming Out 6

Getting to Yes 17

Support for a Mother's Yes. 27

Initiation 37

Medicine Women 47

Life upon the Wicked Stage. 53

To Health. 61

Spring Shadows. 69

The Dying Room 83

Celebrations of Ken 93

Part Two

Reacting to the News 105

Dreams and the Kindness of Strangers 115

Preparations for a Healing. 127

To Brazil. 137

Beyond the Ends of the Earth. 147

Extremely High-Tech Medicine 157

Bone Marrow Summer 165

One Hundred Days Plus 173

Dancing on the Edge 181

Saying Good-Bye 193

Midwifery Again. 205

Ashes 209

The Grandmother Ceremony 219

After Words 223

PREFACE

People would often say to me, "This isn't the way it's supposed to be, children dying before their parents." They said it when my thirty-one-year-old son, Kenneth, died of AIDS and again, seven years later, when my forty-two-year-old daughter, Corinne, died of breast cancer. When Corinne died, I got a phone call from my cousin, who had lost her own daughter in a car accident twenty years before. "This shouldn't be happening to you," she said, in an effort to comfort me. When I asked whom it should be happening to, she said, "Someone who hasn't already lost a child."

But I prefer not to think this way. When I am in that place of questioning the circumstances of my own life, I picture the gravestones in the historical cemeteries my history-buff father took us to visit as children. We kids would run from gravestone to gravestone, doing the math and discovering children our own ages or younger buried there. I remind myself that it's only in recent generations and in a country as fortunate as our own that parents can expect to raise all their children and to predecease them.

So I set out to write about my experiences as a mother who has lost two of her three adult children to horrific diseases. I voluntarily reentered those years of anxiety, trauma, and hope to better understand what transpired there. I realized that those of us who survived have been profoundly changed, and so I have written partly for my own healing and partly to share with others the learning and strength I discovered. Many people did not understand my spending so much time writing about this, especially my husband, Richard, whose style of grieving was entirely different. Rich and I finally came to an understanding several years into this project.

Rich and I are both behavioral health professionals. We share a conviction that many mental health problems are caused by a lack of connection to people's spiritual selves. In our work and for our own personal development, we use the community- building tools of dance, song, and story. In the jargon of our professions, this is called using the arts for individual and social transformation. For ten years we founded and co-directed a behavioral health care clinic called Iatreia Institute for the Healing Arts. This was the name of the clinic from 1987-1997 until we were purchased by Corphealth. Then it became Iatreia, Inc. You'd think that the experience of our professional careers and the synchronicity of our shared beliefs would have given us some special insight into each other's grief. Not so.

Five summers ago, Rich sent me off to participate in a writers' workshop with the comment, "I hope someday you will find something more pleasant to write about."

When I returned from the writers' workshop in Iowa City, held a couple of weeks after the town had suffered a significant flood, I brought back two empty sandbags, like the thousands of bags of sand stacked as barricades against the rising waters. My empty sandbags had been decorated and made into handbags by artists in the community and sold to raise money to help the local Habitat for Humanity fund the cleanup efforts. At home I laid out my decorated sandbags alongside a folder of my writing. "My writings are *my* sandbags," I told Rich. "We have to make art out of what happens to us, or at least something useful, and we don't get to pick what that is."

People have asked me how I've survived all the tragedy and loss in my life. Perhaps I've written the stories of my journeys with my children, other family members, and my best friend to answer that question for myself. Witnessing how hard both my children fought to stay alive and all that they were willing to endure to gain more life has defined my grieving process. I never wanted to dishonor them by wasting one moment of whatever precious life I am given.

Like a prospector searching for gold, with the help of my journal, I have panned and sifted through these experiences—of birth, death, and the places in between. I have shaken the sieve in such a way as to uncover, among the dirt, pebbles, and debris, the valuable shiny elements in these stories.

This sifting and sorting has been, like the experiences themselves, tough at times, but also enlightening. I've come to appreciate the many ways that people confront illness, diagnoses, treatment decisions, and, yes, even death, and the many faces and masks of grief. And ultimately, I've come to see the demands made on me as a mother as requiring me to become a warrior mother. In our lifelong mother roles, whether our children are sick or well, young or old, like warriors, we engage wholeheartedly in a cause, and like spiritual warriors, we are asked to use our compassion and wisdom to help our children and ourselves grow and thrive through whatever life sends our way.

PART ONE

COMING OUT

"**I** am the mother of a gay man," I said into a "talking stick" microphone in front of one hundred people. I could hear my heart pounding in my chest. I took a breath before speaking again. The year was 1991; the place Marin County, near San Francisco. As a dancer, I was participating in a ritual/performance to highlight the problem of HIV/AIDS, which by then had become a worldwide pandemic. The people listening to my somewhat shaky voice were gathered in an outdoor courtyard of a high school, where we'd been rehearsing together for five days. The rehearsals would culminate in a public performance directed by one of my most admired mentors, dancer/choreographer Anna Halprin. The workshop participants were adults of various ages and cultures, some having traveled great distances.

"And," I continued, "I don't know how to be his mother." This statement and its implied question were offered under the rules of this contemporary version of an ancient ritual. I could ask the community any question strongly on my mind and heart. I could say anything I wanted, but, as in the indigenous cultures where the talking stick ritual is practiced, it had to be the truth.

The truth was, my difficulties mothering my youngest son, who was twenty-five years old at the time, had been long-standing. I had mothered him through his school years as he struggled with serious learning disabilities, and through the various rituals of his leaving home, returning, and setting out again. Perhaps the accumulation of all those challenges over the years had propelled me to the microphone.

Attempting to mother my youngest adult son had gotten me into working a 12-step program. After years of frenzied attempts to manage Ken's behavior, applying all the reasoned strategies I knew as a therapist and social worker, I started a Codependents Anonymous for Helping Professionals group at our behavioral health care clinic. This group met weekly for four years, and though experiences with clients were occasionally the focus, the support of the group, the twelve steps, and repeated recitations of the serenity prayer were most often applied to the consistent challenges Ken's life kept providing me.

One example: the phone call I got from the Dallas Fire Department. They were conducting an investigation into an alleged arsonist who had bought three gallons of gasoline at a service station in Dallas and had later set fire to a building. Their interest in me was because the credit card used was in my name. It turned out the gas station was close to where Ken lived. Ken had one of my gasoline credit cards along with my permission to use it, but he'd lost it and failed to tell me.

High drama. You've got my attention, Ken.

Once Ken was driving to our clinic with supplies I needed for an open house. When he didn't show up, my mother-worry alarm sounded. Just as the event was starting, I got a phone call. He had been stopped for a broken taillight a few blocks from the clinic. The officer ran a check, found an unpaid ticket that had gone to warrant, and hauled him off to jail.

I consulted a lawyer friend at our event. "Should I let him spend the night in jail?"

He returned my question with another: "How big is he?"

Why would that matter? I wondered.

"I'm not sure the punishment would fit the crime," my friend continued. Suddenly I understood. I shivered as I was assailed by images of Ken being sexually assaulted by bigger, tougher cellmates. The punishment definitely wouldn't fit the crime. Horrified, I paid to get Ken out of jail. As I had done with money in the past, I insisted this was a loan he had to repay, which he always did, and that this was the last time I would get him out.

That wasn't the last time—though there finally was a last time. My husband, Rich, and I were packing for a weeklong vacation on my brother's sailboat around the San Juan Islands near Seattle when I got a call from the jail in Highland Park. This made me smile since Highland Park is a small, wealthy residential enclave completely surrounded by Dallas. Its police station and jail are in the same stone cottage-like structure as its city hall, and the building is barely larger than the homes in the neighborhood. "Leave it to Ken to get picked up in Highland Park," I thought.

But the situation was more complicated. Ken had acquired tickets in several jurisdictions, one as far away as Waco. If he couldn't pay his tickets, and he couldn't without me, he would spend two nights in each of the jails of the counties where his tickets were earned. Oh, great, a tour of the Texas prison system.

I consulted friends and members of my group. I talked with therapists and lawyers, and I prayed for guidance. "What we've been doing isn't working. That's clear," I thought. I fell back on a truism of the Codependents Anonymous program: "I can't change his behavior. I can only change mine."

I went to the police station/jail, paid the $400, and left. Later that day, a contrite, hangdog Ken sat at our kitchen table. He mumbled a feeble "sorry." But I felt I needed to let him in on the process I had used to decide on my action, which on the surface looked like all my other actions.

"No, Ken, I need to apologize to *you*. I'm sorry I got you out of jail yet another time after all those times I said I would never do it again."

Ken looked up from the floor, and his eyes darted side to side as if he were thinking, "What has she come up with now?"

"I'm sorry I got you out because obviously you need to have an experience of jail. And I keep getting in the way of you having that."

Ken tried to interrupt me, but I forged ahead. "I didn't do this for you, Ken. In fact, it was a totally *selfish* decision. I did it for myself.

Rich and I leave for our vacation this weekend, and I would not be able to enjoy myself knowing you were touring the Texas prison system. I realized that what I needed this week is for you to *not* be in a series of jails while I'm on a sailboat far from the mainland."

Now Ken looked as if he'd fallen behind Alice's looking glass alongside a mother who was taking lessons from the Queen of Hearts.

"So, as in our usual arrangements, you will need to pay me back, but I'm not going to say that I'll never get you out of jail again. I don't know what I'll do in the future. I feel unpredictable, even to myself." I began walking out of the room and then turned, as any good actress might, to deliver my exit line.

"The only promise I *will* make is that whatever decision I make the next time, it will come from whatever *I* need at the time."

»»» ▦ «««

Coming to the dance workshop in California at that time and immersing myself in the ritual/performance was what I felt I needed. I'd worked with Anna in the 1970s, when I was in my thirties. Each year, she organized a community ritual on a different theme, and I would get an invitation. Each year I would tell myself, "I'll go one of these years." That particular year, at age fifty-one, I came not drawn by the HIV/AIDS theme but by remembering that Anna was nineteen years older than me, so I'd better stop putting it off.

Yet, with each day of the workshop, I became clearer about how salient its theme was to my life. My concern for my gay son's emotional health, and my simmering fear that he would contract HIV/AIDS in an era when scores of gay men were dying daily of the disease, finally propelled me to the microphone.

"My son seems to be living with a sense of shame." I said. "Hiding from who he is. I try to show him I love him, but it doesn't feel like it helps."

"It's the culture's shame," a tall, burly man called out from the audience, in a voice that needed no microphone. "The whole culture has shame about sexuality, both heterosexual and especially homosexual. This gets internalized by individuals."

I continued: "I told my son about an organization of parents of gays and lesbians. I saw the group marching in New York City on Gay Pride Day. He seemed to appreciate my telling him, 'I will march for you, if that's what's right for you.'" I took a deep breath. "I wish he could be here to feel the support of this community." I told the audience that my husband was flying in for the performance. But after hearing about what we were doing, he wanted to give his plane ticket to our son instead.

A voice from the audience called out, "What is your son's name?"

"Kenneth."

The pause that followed was palpable with his presence.

A woman's voice stated what I was feeling. "It seems like Kenneth just came into the room."

"Well, I'd like to invite Kenneth to come," another male voice in the audience called out. Several voices chimed in, "Yes, we want to meet him."

"But we live in Texas."

"I live in Vermont," a man shouted out.

A slender man in sweatpants and a T-shirt stood up, "I'm from Kentucky. *We* are everywhere."

Participants began shouting out their home states and calling for Ken to come. Then Anna, who knew my husband, suggested, "It would be great if *both* your husband and son could be here."

After the public part of the talking stick ritual, members of the community came up to me privately. A curly-haired man in his early thirties, now living in San Francisco, approached me.

"What you had to say was so powerful for me. My parents in Connecticut were so accepting of my being gay when I came out to them that I had to move all the way across the country to get away from their openness about it! I realize now I couldn't accept their love until I could accept myself."

When a man in his fifties with graying hair came up to thank me for my honesty, I took the opportunity to bring up something that had been bothering me.

"I don't understand the wild sexual exhibitionism some gay men engage in. I know my son is embarrassed by it," I told the man. "And I must admit, it's off-putting to me as well."

"Sexuality for most everybody in our culture is shamed," he explained, "but especially if it's not heterosexual. So much exploration of homosexual sex is done in the backstreets. This can lead to further acting out."

Overhearing our conversation, a woman in her forties added her own experience. "I never really accepted my gayness, and I certainly didn't get any support when I was younger."

Her comment reminded me of how I first learned that my then twenty-one-year-old son was gay. He hadn't come out to his stepfather and me. In fact, it was quite the opposite. He came to me several times during his high school and early college years for support when other people accused him of being gay. Coming home one evening from a seasonal Christmas job at Neiman Marcus, he was in tears. One of the regular sales clerks had confronted him and labeled him homosexual.

"Let's talk," I said as I motioned for Ken to sit down beside me on the sofa in the front bay window of our living room.

"You don't have to let other people define you. You can define yourself," I said, trying to frame this in a way that would give him the most freedom. "I've had to do that myself in my own career." I used the example of being one of only six women professors on a thirty-six-person faculty. "Some of the men professors treated us like we didn't belong there. Even though, of course, most social workers are women."

I pointed out that some people think that being a man means you need to be all about sports. "People see that you're artistic and that you like theater and films, and to them this means you must be gay."

I began to question whether I was doing the right thing when I realized that Ken often lied to me about little things, things that didn't matter—situations when telling the truth would have worked better. One morning, when Ken was about twenty-three years old, as he sat at the kitchen table telling me a story about where he was the night before, I challenged him.

"Ken, I don't believe what you're telling me. I don't know the truth, but I know this isn't it."

He looked down into his cereal bowl in silence.

"I try to think about what it is you don't want me to know." And standing in the middle of the kitchen, I took a wild guess: "That you were with a *man* last night?" By the expression on his face, I knew I'd stumbled onto the truth. I'd outed him.

I wondered how I didn't know sooner. But a year later, when he talked with me about his own homophobia, how he didn't want to be gay, I realized I couldn't know until he did.

"So let me get this clear. You want me to fly to San Francisco for the weekend and *you'll* pay all expenses?" Ken said when I phoned to invite him to the performance.

"Yep, that's the invitation." I also mentioned that his sister, Corinne, and her husband, Bill, would be in the San Francisco area on vacation, so they might meet up with us some time over the weekend.

He hung up, promising to think about it. A few minutes later he called back, and his voice quivered with excitement when he said he would come. Ken had gotten into his own Codependents Anonymous group by then, and he'd talked my offer over with his sponsor. "Jeff thinks it's a great opportunity for me—and he wants to know if you and Rich would consider 'adopting' him so he could come too."

>>> ▪ <<<

Kenneth arrived at the high school in Marin in time to catch the end of our rehearsal. We dancers were sweaty and tired, but most everyone became part of a joyful welcoming committee for him. His blue eyes sparkled and his boyish face lit up as people shook his hands. My chest swelled with pride as people asked me to personally introduce them.

"We're so glad you could make it," they said, their affirming smiles proclaiming, "Welcome to San Francisco. How long can you stay?"

Audience members were beginning to find seats in the bleachers as I walked around the high school gymnasium, now transformed into a ritual space. Richard, Kenneth, Corinne, and Bill would all be witnesses. I tried to dismiss the trepidation in my stomach, having ritual and real life intersecting so dramatically. I wondered what my family would make of what they were about to see, especially Corinne and Bill. Some of my uneasiness came from the strong link between HIV/AIDS and homosexuality at that time, and my knowledge that the doctrine of Corinne and Bill's church rejected homosexuality. Corinne had expressed her worry to her brother that he wouldn't be able to go to heaven if he lived as a homosexual. When Ken and I had spoken of this issue, he'd smiled and said, "Don't worry about it, Mom. She doesn't think you and Rich are going to heaven either."

I remembered a way that Anna liked to describe ritual, and repeating her phrase soothed my jangled insides. "Ritual is love made visible." As I heard the drums and flutes warming up, I took that as my mantra. "Ritual is love made visible."

As the rabbi, the priest, the minister, and the Native American shaman were reviewing their opening remarks, I walked slowly around the gym, pausing at the first of four elaborately decorated altars. We dancers had been directed by Anna to spend some time meditating at each altar before the ritual began. The altars represented the four directions of the Native American worldview. Lush greenery and art objects created a picture of each direction: flowers in bud form honored the East, where new light comes from; blooms of harvest gold and stalks of wheat depicted the West, where the light goes; full blooming red-and-yellow bouquets of flowers represented the South, where life comes from. The North, in white and dark relief, the place where death comes from, seemed to draw me with a special magnetism. I paused

COMING OUT

longer before its altar, noticing the smooth texture of the bony animal skull surrounded by a snowy white barren landscape, as in a Georgia O'Keeffe painting. For the first time, I allowed myself to fully feel the fear for my son's life that I had carried from the time I first learned he was gay. At this time in history, HIV/AIDS and homosexuality had become inseparably linked. And HIV/AIDS had become inseparably linked to death.

Out of the fear came a quiet inner voice: "To continue to be the mother to our children, we must walk with them, whatever walk they walk."

The part of the ritual I still remember twenty years later is the Warrior Dance. The hundred-person cast had been divided into five lines of twenty people, standing shoulder to shoulder. Each person's arms were raised as though lifting weights overhead, and everyone's hands were clasped with their neighbors' hands on either side. As the drums signaled the first line to advance, each person, standing with feet broadly apart, looked to the left and stepped to the right. In a synchronicity that rivaled the Rockettes of Radio City Music Hall fame, the dancers lifted their left knees waist-high while pulling their arms in a downward thrust and expelling their breath to create a deep sound of "HO."

Used by practitioners of self-defense systems, the "HO" sound comes from the center of the abdomen, the *dan tien*, or what Anna calls the "red zone." Its deep resonance strikes fear in the opponent and leaves no doubt of the warrior's unwavering commitment to progress forward. Each line of warriors continued the movement: left, "HO," right, "HO," left, "HO," right, "HO," advancing forward toward the audience. The drums continued their beat. As each line replaced the previous line, the first line circled back to the rear to become the new recruits.

With each movement and sound, my sense of power grew—the firm reverberations in my belly, the hum of air coming up the back of my throat, the deep guttural sounds the movement forced out of my mouth. As my feet pounded the floor in rhythm to the drums, I felt connected to the core of the earth. As my hands kept connection to the persons on either side of me, I felt connected to all the shamans, ancient and modern, who were marshaling the powers of collective action to confront this challenge. We were warriors repelling this pandemic threat to our communities, this potential threat to my own son.

After the performance, Rich and Ken, Bill and Corinne found me in the crowd of performers and audience members. Hugging my family, I felt the love that ritual demonstrates that Anna spoke about. I didn't get much chance to find out what Corinne and Bill really thought about the experience, as they declined to have dinner with us. Corinne was fighting off the nausea of the early months of her pregnancy and needed to get to bed early as they planned to head off to the wine country early the next morning.

The next day, Ken and I took Rich to the airport and then walked along the beach at Point Reyes National Seashore. As a half-dozen hawks rode the wind currents overhead, I told Ken how frightened I'd been for him since I'd first learned he was gay. "The ritual got me in touch with that fear," I told him, "yet at the same time, it's given me confidence that I can walk with you on whatever path your life takes you."

Ken reassured me: "Don't worry, Mom. I'm taking care of myself, and I plan to keep on doing that."

GETTING TO YES

I was mad: my default reaction when anything big and negative happens in my life. But this time I was *really* mad. Two years after the ritual, a couple of weeks before Christmas 1993, I was standing in the main lobby of the hospital, just outside the cafeteria, with its smell of burnt coffee and greasy French fries, talking to my ex-husband, George. Dwarfed by the high ceilings, we stood amid hyper polished, antiseptic corridors, struggling to have a private conversation. We'd been divorced eighteen years by then, longer than we'd been married. Our son Ken had been admitted to the hospital the day before with pneumonia, and although the hospital ward was currently hosting people with six types of pneumonia, the doctor had already expressed strong suspicion that Ken's could be *pneumocystis pneumonia*. In 1993 that was the working definition of AIDS, and George and I knew that.

I pushed the hair back out of my eyes as I attempted to make sense of this frightening possibility. "Of course, he *told* me he was taking care of himself," I blurted out at George. "It's not like we never talked about it." I could hear the fear underneath the anger in my own voice.

George, slender, six foot three, with a full head of grayish-white hair, looked like he always looked when I got emotional: stoic and distant. Pacing the narrow hallway, he gestured into the hospital cafeteria.

"It's a disgrace," he barked. "The only thing on their menu for vegetarians is a dried-out salad bar." George, a recovering alcoholic and triple-bypass survivor, had determinedly not allowed any alcohol, fat, or meat to cross his lips since his surgery five years before.

"How is it we get to go straight to the head of the class?" I spit the words into the atmosphere. "No ten years of symptom-free HIV status, no time to try alternative approaches to staying healthy." I thought about the university courses I'd taught for social workers in health care and my article "Moving Beyond the Medical Model: What Social Workers Need to Know." I knew things that strengthened the immune system: herbs and detoxifying regimens, biofeedback and other body-mind approaches. But aloud I said, "Nothing I know will be of any use now."

This conversation wasn't much different from many others in the thirty years we'd known one another. George seemed to be studying the patterns on the floor. "When are these people gonna wise up? They pay no attention to nutrition and then wonder why people get sick."

"And where was the Centers for Disease Control?" I raged. "Why didn't they pay more attention when this disease first came on the scene?"

Finally looking me in the eye, former radio broadcaster George said in his most professional newscaster cadence: "They ignored it because it was discovered in gay men."

>>> ■ <<<

These themes and images circled around inside my head, on and off during the daytime, and more persistently at night, when I lay awake reliving the recent past. Earlier in December, the weather in Texas had been cold and damp, the kind of damp that seemed to seep into your bones. Lots of people sniffled with colds, but Ken's cough just wouldn't get better. One evening when he was on his way to work, his black wool cap pulled down over his thick brown hair, I suggested he get to a doctor for something stronger than Nyquil. He climbed into the front seat of his small truck, its front grille decorated with a battery-operated Christmas wreath. "Don't worry, Mom," he said as he waved good-bye. The tiny wreath lights blinked on and off into the dusky sky.

When my mother-worry couldn't stand it anymore, I'd arranged an appointment with a physician I knew and asked George to go with Ken because of my work schedule. The next thing I knew, Ken was in the hospital being treated for pneumonia. The hospital tests regarding Ken's HIV status weren't back yet when the physicians released him to our home. They'd prescribed bed rest and Bactrim, just in case he was HIV positive.

Ken, George, Rich, and I had planned to meet Kevin, our older son, and spend the Christmas holidays in Nebraska, where Corinne lived with her family. Instead, I celebrated Christmas running up and down the stairs attending to Ken with some help from his two fathers, step-dad Rich and bio-dad George, who slept in his RV, parked in our driveway.

Most nights, I'd fall into bed too exhausted to sleep, wishing I'd taken more after my mother, a registered nurse. I'd think of her red-headed take-charge persona and ask, "What would Mother do in this situation?"

It wasn't that my nurse mother had all the answers about taking care of her own children. I recalled that when I was in labor with my first child, Corinne, Mother had wanted to help. But as a labor and delivery room nurse, she had a very different relationship to Western medicine than I had. I had tried to demedicalize my pregnancy and delivery, being among the first wave of women in Western culture that told doctors that having a baby and becoming a mother was not a disease, but a natural process. Following in the footsteps of an older woman I admired, my husband and I took childbirth preparation courses so I could have a natural childbirth. With the popularity of that approach now, it's hard to imagine how difficult it was at the time to find medical personnel who'd be cooperative. My intent was not to squat down in a field for the birth but to have all the advantages of modern medicine's technology standing by.

I was forced to change doctors twice, once when we moved to Michigan from New York and again when the Michigan doctor finally admitted that his version of natural childbirth did not include spouses being present.

"Your husband can be there when you're not in active labor," the doctor had told me three weeks before my due date. I told him, "I plan to stay home when I'm not in active labor." I luckily found a doctor willing to allow my husband to assist me in being fully present for the birth.

But Mother's role was more difficult to define. According to friends who'd had her on their team when they were in labor, she was the best. But she'd rarely seen a labor and delivery without anesthesia, and never one that purposely set out in that direction. I saw, even in the dim labor room light, her switching back and forth between her role as a nurse and her role as my mother, fighting back tears, upset to the point of occasionally leaving the room in distress. Of course, I was too preoccupied to comfort her. Later, we both agreed: standing by feeling helpless while I appeared to be suffering made this process harder on her than on me. For my next two births, she stayed home and dutifully cared for her grandchildren.

>>> ■ <<<

After sixteen-plus hours of labor and the birth of my daughter, a young twenty-something male intern was bending over my hospital bed. His voice reverberating with disgust that sounded like accusation, he said, "She looks like she's been hit by shrapnel."

Pushing on my flaccid, sore abdomen, the chief doctor enlightened the cadre of white-coated male residents surrounding us about stretch marks. "This is a particularly dramatic example of *striae gravidarum*, a scarring on the skin due to pregnancy. Note the purple lines and red marks caused not just by the stretching of the skin but by hormonal changes and genetics. They will lighten a bit with time but never completely disappear."

I was not yet twenty-three years old. I was elated at my good fortune, having delivered a healthy baby girl, yet I was also thinking, "I'm now marked for life as someone who has given life. No bikini bathing suits for me (and just when I was getting up the nerve to wear one). My dancer's body will now require a cover-up."

In the past forty years, I've gotten a fuller appreciation for the "stretch marks" that mothering brings. And I was about to find out for myself how hard it is to be in that mother-of-the-patient role.

Help came when five women from my women's spirituality group invited Rich and me to a pipe ceremony on behalf of Ken and our family. This ritual was familiar to us through our friend Glenda, a women's studies teacher with Native American ancestry. She led women's spirituality groups at her retreat center in East Texas. Most group members had grown up in various mainstream religious traditions, but the Native American practices Glenda taught us allowed us to transcend our differences and to pray together in community.

Rich and I assembled with friends in my friend Carol's living room and established a sacred space, with candles and a bouquet of fresh flowers in the center of our circle. Each person said out loud a wish or prayer to place in the pipe. The pipe carriers put a small piece of tobacco in the clay pipe to represent each prayer. Tobacco is sacred in native traditions, its smoke connecting heaven and earth. The pipe is said to contain everything that is, has been, or will be: "All My Relations," as the native people say, reminding us that we are related to all that is. What we might call good or bad, friend or enemy, hope or despair, health or illness—all dualities are in the pipe.

The pipe was passed around the circle, and each of us took into our own bodies "all that is" and exhaled the representational smoke back into the cosmos.

One of only a couple of men at the ceremony, our dear friend Randall, told a story, a parable that has stayed with me all the years since:

A man was running away from a hungry tiger. The man ran so fast that he ran over the side of a steep cliff. On the way down, he grabbed with both hands a branch that was protruding from the side of the mountain. This left him hanging on for dear life, suspended between two undesirable realities. When he looked up, he saw the tiger looking down at him. Looking down below him, he saw another ferocious tiger at the bottom of the culvert, looking up at him. He couldn't return to where he'd been, and he couldn't allow himself to drop to the ground. The next moment he noticed a beautiful, plump, rosy-red strawberry within easy reach of one of his hands. Taking a deep breath and hanging on with only one hand now, he picked the strawberry and ate it with complete enjoyment, licking every last bit of juice dripping down his fingers and hand.

>>> ■ <<<

After Ken had been at our house for about a week, he started complaining of itching behind his ears. Upon a closer look, I discovered flaking red skin covering a great deal of his upper body. When I took his temperature, it showed a fever of 101 degrees. I became determined to take him back to the hospital, disregarding the advice of Ken's two dads. George cautioned, "Don't overreact." I disregarded him.

Just driving onto the hospital property brought immediate relief to my mother- worry. I dropped Ken at the emergency entrance and circling the parking ramp, I told myself, "Whatever's causing the rash, the professionals are in the building—help is close at hand."

While we waited in the sparsely furnished emergency waiting area, the police delivered a man on a gurney with a gunshot wound, a couple of teenagers were triaged after an automobile accident, and a social worker arrived with an unidentified newborn found on the doorstep of a convent. I'm ashamed to admit that I welcomed these dramatic ER distractions; they kept my mother-worry otherwise occupied.

Eventually, Ken's bright head-to-toe rash got us into a small examining room, where a nurse took some history and a doctor looked him over. When the doctor learned that Ken had been a patient at the hospital the prior week, he left to look up his hospital record. Returning with the file under his arm, he perched on a stool and, resting the paperwork on a table, began reading out loud items from Ken's record, including, "HIV status, positive." He looked up, saw the expression on our faces, and realized we were hearing this information for the first time.

"No one called you?" Shaking his head, he said, "I thought you knew."

His words fell like lead. We'd hoped and prayed for any one of the other five kinds of pneumonia the hospital patients had been infected with over the holidays. Without knowing what each type of pneumonia entailed, any one would have been a reprieve. Though my son was twenty-seven, looking at his crumpled figure, huddled on the narrow cot in the windowless room, he seemed a very young child, wide-eyed and frightened. His eyes begged me to protect him. I told myself to remain calm and strong for his sake. My mind went to my women's spirituality group, remembering they were praying for us. This was definitely a moment to call on help from other realms.

The ER doctor admitted he knew next to nothing about AIDS and that he would have to consult with an infectious disease specialist. He asked if I knew anyone in particular. If so, we could contact that person to follow up later on Ken's case. Energized by a tangible task, I began making phone calls. Using my social work contacts, I located a doctor in Dallas with a stellar reputation in the infectious diseases field who agreed to take Ken on as a patient. He spoke with the ER doctor, and they determined that Ken was having an allergic reaction to the Bactrim, so he was taken off it. By the time we left the hospital, we had the promise of an appointment the following week with the Dallas specialist. The only thing we knew about him besides his reputation in my social work circles was that he sounded nice on the phone.

My sleep patterns only got worse when it was confirmed that Ken had AIDS. In the middle of the night, I would do the math. Given the usual course of the disease, a ten-year period between initial infection and the onset of serious symptoms, Ken must have become infected at eighteen or nineteen years of age. While he was still in high school? Or shortly afterward?

I called my friend Cynthia in California for support. We'd met a year earlier, and I'd come to trust what she calls her body wisdom; she was teaching me how to trust mine. Cynthia was a dancer and minister, the cofounder of InterPlay, an improvisational system that involves dance, song, and storytelling. Now the centerpiece of my work life, InterPlay is sometimes used as an expressive art therapy, sometimes to create transformational performances. I adopted InterPlay immediately upon discovering it, since it brought together so much of what I'd done in my life as a professional dancer, social worker, therapist, and teacher.

Cynthia let me rant a bit on the phone about Ken's diagnosis before cautioning, "Don't get caught up in categories."

"What do you mean?"

"A diagnosis is a label, a category, but it rarely defines an experience. You and Ken get to do that." She told me about people she knew who had AIDS and were doing well, living their lives with a new appreciation for its gifts.

Then she said, "Find a way to say yes to it." This message hit me like the proverbial slap in the face.

"What?"

"Find a way to say yes to it."

Yes to a life-threatening disease? At the time, that seemed more than a tall order; it seemed impossible. But somehow, in the depths of myself, I knew she was right. Life was asking this of my son, and if I was to share in his life, it was asking it of me.

As often happens with rituals, it is only later that I realize their power and deeper meanings. After my discussion with Cynthia, I thought again about the pipe ceremony, and I realized that the pipe ceremony was a way of practicing saying yes. Yes to what has been, what is now, and what is to come. And looking again at Randall's story, which I have gone back to many times in the years since, helps me remember that the present moment is all we really have, so savoring its gifts is a way of living in the ongoing Big Yes!

SUPPORT FOR A
MOTHER'S YES

I had written a book for professional and family caregivers years before my own dramatic need for such advice in my own life, so I knew the importance of taking care of myself. I knew that to be able to support Ken as he was dealing with this life-threatening disease, I needed to do everything I could to stay healthy myself. I also had the example of my own mother and her failure to thrive during and after the ordeal she went through with her son. My younger brother, Kenny, had disappeared a few weeks before his twenty-sixth birthday.

Kenny was born just before my ninth birthday, and he was everybody's favorite, the family's "golden child." We four older kids fought over who would get to hold him, take him for walks, and sit by him when he was old enough to sit at the children's table. In his teens, Kenny had explored being a priest, but before his disappearance, he was living in a tepee, involved with an Indian tribe in New Mexico as it reinstituted the Sun Dance festival. I remember finding his involvement with a Native American tribe amazing, since my job at the time, in my mid-thirties at the School of Social Work, involved working with Native American and Mexican American communities in the western part of Nebraska. It seemed we both had an affinity for the First Peoples, although our mixed Irish, Scottish, and English ancestry didn't connect with them genetically, as far as we knew.

The sixteen months of not knowing what happened to my brother Kenny was difficult for all the members of our family, but it was excruciating for our mother. She imagined scenarios that could explain his disappearance yet would allow him to still be alive. Perhaps he was in a prison in Mexico, having been found with a marijuana cigarette in his pocket. Perhaps he was in an accident without any identification on him and he hadn't contacted us because he had amnesia. She lit candles, prayed the rosary, and sent money and prayer requests to monasteries and convents, beseeching them to pray for her son's safe return home.

In the second autumn after his disappearance, two hunters found a body in a national forest in New Mexico. My parents were notified and asked to send dental records, and they confirmed the body as my brother's. The autopsy report determined the cause of death to be a bullet, delivered at close range to the back of his head.

Our family held a funeral and burial service with his remains in the town where he grew up. But then, within six months of the funeral, nearly every remaining family member experienced a major illness. One sister had esophageal surgery; another made a middle-of-the-night trip to the emergency room with an ovary that had burst for no explainable medical reason. A brother had stomach problems, and I had colitis-type symptoms that persisted for several years. Healthy before and since, our father had a bout with kidney stones, and Mother had a heart attack. While teaching a university course on family systems therapy, I drew a diagram of these events, and, looking at the blackboard, it hit me. Our family was one body, and we each carried the pain of Kenny's loss in a different organ.

We all recovered except Mother. Looking back, it's clear she never survived the death of her son. She remained in ill health to the end of her life, dying eight years later of pancreatic cancer. Mother struggled with but could never reconcile how her peace-loving son Kenny, a conscientious objector who did alternative service in a hospital during the Vietnam War, could have died violently. After my son Ken's diagnosis,

I returned to this sense of a family as one body. I prayed not only for him but for myself, his two fathers, his brother and sister, and all those whose lives he touched.

>>> ■ <<<

Seated on the edge of the examination table for a routine physical exam, costumed in the usual skimpy patient gown, I began telling the family's story to my own physician. "My son Ken has been diagnosed with AIDS." Reaching for a tissue from the box on the side table, I filled in some of the details. "His T cell count is 293. They prescribed Bactrim to prevent pneumonia, but he's allergic to it."

My personal physician was a woman about my age whom I called by her first name. A brilliant scientist who had been a nun in her former life, Mary Ann understood that what's wrong with a patient might not be discernible through a physical examination. So although it was not a procedure reimbursed by an insurance company, she listened intently as I spoke about what was going on in my life.

After saying how sorry she was, Mary Ann told me that about 30 percent of the population is allergic to sulfa drugs, but the good news was that Ken could be desensitized to it. "It works like allergy shots work. You receive a small amount of the substance repeatedly, and your body builds up a tolerance to it."

Mary Ann also mentioned a physician friend at the medical school who was doing research on the juice of the aloe vera plant as a potential treatment for AIDS. She thought it might be worth looking into, especially since the juice was being manufactured in Dallas. She'd heard of another physician in Denver whose son had been diagnosed with AIDS several years before who sponsored a national conference, AIDS, Medicine & Miracles. The conference was held yearly to share medical, alternative, and complementary treatments and strategies for staying healthy while living with HIV/AIDS.

Coming from that appointment, I felt some small encouragement.

At least I had some things to offer Ken besides the AZT that the infectious disease doctor had prescribed, which was making him sick to his stomach. Ken was familiar with the aloe vera plant since we, like many Texas families, always had one in our kitchen. You break a piece off the cactus-like plant with pointy green leaves, squeeze the clear slimy substance onto a burnt finger, and voila! The pain vanishes. It had always seemed like magic, and given the state of the art of AIDS treatment at the time, we weren't against reaching for magic, let alone a few miracles.

So it didn't take much for me to talk Ken into driving to a nearby suburb to get some of the juice. We drove to a mostly deserted, one-story office complex in the nearby city of Grand Prairie. When no one answered the bell, we tried the door and it opened. We called out, but no one answered. As it was rather dark inside, and getting darker outside, it felt scary to enter. But having gone this far, we entered.

No one was around. Only a couple of desks piled with papers and some cardboard boxes strewn about. Finally, a middle-aged man in shirtsleeves emerged from the back room. He apologized for not hearing us come in.

He looked pretty suspicious, putting jugs of colorless liquid with handmade labels into cartons for transporting. Ken said later that our trip reminded him of stories he'd heard of people crossing the border into Mexico in search of drugs or some wacky treatment that would be illegal in the States.

After the man helped us load the car with a case of the elixir and we were on our way, Ken said, "I hope no one stops us at the border into Arlington and we have to explain what we're carrying in our trunk."

Ken did drink the juice on a somewhat frequent basis. It had to be refrigerated, so he kept a jug in his apartment refrigerator, and we had one in ours. It seemed to help with the upset stomach he got from the AZT but didn't prove to make the real difference we were looking for in our desperation, a cure for this disease.

In the years since, I've seen many people go to the places where Ken and I went when the type or stage of their disease surpassed the proven expertise of Western scientific medicine. The desire for more years of life can initiate a modern-day version of the search for the Holy Grail—whether a Google search or an actual trip to Mexico or China.

>>> ■ <<<

Shortly after the diagnosis, Ken took a class at the AIDS Outreach Center in Fort Worth. He would always come home uplifted by the support he received in the groups and from his one-on-one counseling. But in contrast to the openness of the center environment, the counselors' primary advice to Ken, in relation to the rest of the world, was to keep his HIV status a secret. I remember him telling me, "They said if your best friend works where you do, don't even tell *him*." This advice felt like a recipe for isolation to my social worker brain, but I understood that it no doubt came from the many cases where people had lost their jobs when employers became aware of their HIV status. The agency had lawyers to help people fight such actions, but it suggested that the better path would be to avoid the situation altogether. Ken didn't want or need a lawsuit; he just wanted to keep his job as a hotel concierge. As important as his keeping his job was, though, I knew we family members needed support. So we shared our situation discreetly with our most trusted friends.

In late January 1994, we again held our winter women's spirituality retreat at my friend Carol's ranch in North Texas. Winter was the only season we could safely share the rocky ranch terrain with the local snakes. Reportedly, they slept through the cold weather, and for sure our favorite meditation spot among ancient rocks was theirs in all other seasons.

The bunkhouse was simple—a kitchen at one end of a large room that held mismatched sofas and a few chairs around a stone fireplace. The walls were covered with maps, newspaper accounts of the land's history, and four stuffed heads of deer, former residents of the property. The "bunks" lay in another small room, used by ranch hands during other seasons. A dozen of us women slept on cots or on the sofas, and some braver souls chose outside tents or the beds of their trucks or SUVs.

I felt so grateful to have this group of women in my life and the opportunity to get together each season in a ceremonial way. After being pushed out of the Catholic Church of my youth, I longed for a place for ritual and community, a place where being a woman was not a "less-than" status. During Pope John's brief reign, in the early 1960s, when the Roman Catholic Church seemed to be growing in the same ways I was, I had high hopes for the church and for my place as a woman in it. But in the backlash that prevailed against women, I could no longer sit in the pew beside my young daughter listening to sermons and observing ceremonial practices that dishonored women.

This retreat was our fourth winter at the ranch, so our routines were fairly established. We came on Friday afternoon and left Sunday after lunch. In between, we created altars with pictures of the people important in our lives. We used music, dance, stories, and poems to express our dreams, fears, and triumphs. Glenda did some teaching from the women's studies curriculum she'd developed over the years, covering Jungian archetypes, the symbols and stories of goddesses, and indigenous wisdom from her Native American ancestors and teachers.

I'd arrived early to help build the structure for a Native American sweat lodge ritual. Carol's husband and some of the ranch hands had cut some young green branches and soaked them in water for easy bending. We women bent the softened branches and tied them together to create an igloo-shaped frame. After digging a fire pit in the center of our structure and one nearby to heat the rocks, we decorated the branches with prayer ties, little strips of cloth filled with tobacco and tied to the frame, each representing a particular prayer. Next we placed blankets over the frame to create a dome-shaped tent to contain the heat and steam.

Once the ritual began, we took turns entering the lodge in small groups. The rocks heated in the outside fire pit had been transported by a shovel to the inside pit. We huddled in the moist darkness around the center pit, first being warmed by the steam from water we'd poured over the hot rocks, then sweltering and sweating onto our towels as we sat on benches or squatted close to the ground. We prayed individually and together for ourselves, for people we knew, and for the strength to serve life.

The next morning, sitting beside Carol on one of the bunkhouse sofas near the fireplace, tears welled up in my throat. Primed by the experience of the sweat lodge, the extended effort of holding it together through my son Ken's AIDS diagnosis, and the weeks of taking care of him when he had pneumonia, I blinked back the tears filling my eyes. Ken was doing relatively well by this time, back at work and living in his own apartment. But I struggled to compose myself. I thought, "If I get started crying, I will never stop."

As a child, I was not permitted to cry in public. If I started to cry when we had company, I would be sent into another room and not allowed to rejoin the family until I could behave "normally." I still have a vivid memory of standing against the tiled wall in the bathroom alongside big blue towels hanging on the towel rack. I would nuzzle my face into the terry cloth and rely on it to muffle my sobs. Then, after a time, I'd wipe the tears and snot from my face, regain my composure, and join my family. This didn't seem like such a terrible punishment at the time, but I realized later that, in our family, crying in public had been shamed. And this has somewhat negative consequences for grieving.

So here in the bunkhouse with my woman friends, I continued to struggle to compose myself. As tears were occasionally breaking through, despite my efforts, I continued to apologize to Carol, who was seated next to me. She would have none of it. She put her arms around me and held me as I gave myself over to the tears I'd been withholding.

Carol said, "I honor your tears. These are sacred tears. A mother's tears are sacred."

These words came to me as new information, a balm to the pain in my mother's heart. As Carol held me, I allowed myself to cry until my tears were spent. And it didn't take as long as I'd imagined. A few minutes later, Carol blotted my face with Kleenex, which members of the women's group ever afterward called "sacred tissues". After emerging from the sweat lodge and crying in Carol's sheltering arms, I felt cleansed in my body and, for the first time in a long time, at peace in my soul.

>>> ■ <<<

The AIDS, Medicine & Miracles conference that Mary Ann had told me about was to be held at a hotel near the airport in San Francisco. Once home, I began making arrangements for our family to attend. Richard and I would fly with Ken from Texas, his brother, Kevin, would come up from LA, and George would drive down from Oregon. Only Corinne would miss this gathering; she had recently delivered her second baby.

When we arrived, Ken was not feeling well. He'd regained some weight after recovering from the pneumonia, but he seemed lethargic and depressed. He stayed in his hotel room, missing the conference offerings on the first day. I thought, "I didn't pay to fly you out here so you could stay in your room," but I managed to avoid saying that to him.

I met a woman in a small caregivers' group at the conference who was an acupuncture practitioner. She claimed to have had some success with alleviating medication-induced symptoms for people with AIDS. "I'd be happy to give your son a treatment and see if it will help," she offered. I wasn't sure he'd be willing, but I went upstairs to ask. I probably begged a little, and so he agreed to try it. His headache and stomach upset were gone almost immediately after the treatment. This was a tremendous blessing. Not only did the acupuncture allow him to participate more fully in the rest of the conference, but later he returned to it often to alleviate symptoms caused by the various medications he took throughout the next several years.

Coming to the HIV/AIDS conference from the "culture of silence" recommended by our local AIDS outreach group, we were relieved to hear so many people talking out loud about AIDS. I still remember a Native American healer saying in one of the presentations, "A disease that is kept a secret cannot heal." We social workers have our own version of how secrets operate: We often say, "Families are only as sick as their secrets," which was why I had to alter a bit the advice we had received from the local AIDS organization.

Conference participants were people who had been diagnosed (mostly gay men and a few former IV drug users), professional caregivers, practitioners of various alternative treatment modalities (acupuncturists, massage therapists, nutritionists), physicians, researchers, and an occasional friend of someone with AIDS. We were shocked and saddened to learn during the last session of the conference that of the 250 or so attendees, we were the only family who'd accompanied a patient. Many of the young men came up to Ken and told him how they envied the support of his family. I found it hard to imagine that parents wouldn't want to support their children. I wondered if these participants had told their families about their diagnosis or even that they were gay.

People often had trouble determining Ken's age, and that was true for me as well. At times he seemed younger than his years, playful and inventive; at other times older, sensitive and astute. Ken was fourteen when we were living in Texas and I was teaching at a university and working to finish my dissertation. He often stopped by my office on his way home from school, but one particular afternoon, when I returned from a meeting, I saw he had already been there and gone. A prominently displayed note on my desk—"I want it. I've earned it. I deserve it. I can do it," a gift from a professional woman who had told me that this mantra helped her finish her dissertation—was now displayed on each of the four walls of my office.

I recognized Ken's handwriting in the four copies of the message, displayed so that no matter what direction I looked, as I swiveled around in my office chair, the note's encouraging message would smile back at me. "I want it. I've earned it. I deserve it. I can do it." I thought at the time, "This kid really understands the problem, and he's come up with a great solution."

As our family members said good-bye to one another after the conference, to return to Texas and Oregon and Southern California, I realized how important it was for me to find some way to do for Ken what he had done for me—so that no matter where he looked, he would receive the encouragement to keep going on his path toward healing.

>>> ▓ <<<

By the following Christmas, Ken looked healthy and happy again. His life was going well. He had a new job, and he brought someone special to our family Christmas celebration. He'd met Les at a health club. Les knew about Ken's HIV status and seemed accepting and supportive. I felt especially grateful for Les because one of my strongest fears for my son was that, with this diagnosis, he would never find someone to love and be loved in return. I knew that was something he wanted and that I wanted for him, along with a much longer life than the statistics would encourage us to expect.

INITIATION

In the fall of 1993, six months before Ken's diagnosis, Rose, my best friend of nearly twenty years, and I were walking on the beach at Corpus Christi, Texas. I remember the sensations of wet sand on my feet and cool water splashing at my ankles. The gentle sea breeze seemed to pick up speed as low-flying seagulls chirped overhead. In the calmness of the moment, Rose turned to me and said, "I've been diagnosed with breast cancer." Now I understood why she had called from Nebraska, saying she needed to go to the beach "this week, if possible." The Gulf erased our footprints in the wet sand as we walked in silence for some distance. I needed to steady the churning sensations in my gut before asking for details about what the doctors were recommending.

Rose seemed unruffled. "I'll be fine. I'm scheduled for a mastectomy when I get back. That way, I'll be recovered in time for Jill's wedding."

Rose and I had met when I interviewed her for a job to assist Nebraska school districts with Title IX, the legislation that opened up sports for women and girls. "After my fourth child was born severely retarded," Rose told me during the interview, "I had to let go of my shyness, get out of the house, and become her voice. Friends and I went everywhere with empty suitcases, bringing back literature about any good ideas being done anywhere for disabled people. I've done children and the disabled. Now I'm ready to go to work for women," she said with a sparkly smile, dark eyes shining.

While Rose talked, I attempted to fill out the form my university colleague and I had devised to impartially compare job candidates. As she described her experience as a PE teacher and her training with Saul Alinsky, the legendary community organizer, I gave up on that form. I knew no matter what her score, we would hire her. And through the years, I've felt extremely blessed to be friends with this lively, positive activist whose high-school-age son once said of her, "In the disguise of a slightly overweight middle-aged housewife beats the heart of a radical."

In her customary "no need to make a big deal out of it" way, Rose did what the doctors recommended. After the surgery, no radiation or chemotherapy was deemed necessary. She told me the doctor said, "Take these pills every day for the next five years, and you'll be fine." She made it to her daughter's wedding as planned. But a couple of years later, it wasn't fine. On another trip to the beach, Rose was limping from pain in her hip. When she got home, we learned the cancer had spread to her bones.

>>> ■ <<<

One Saturday in late August 1995, my husband tracked me down at the nail salon. A man on a mission, his ball-cap-topped six-foot frame couldn't have seemed more out of place as he approached the small manicure table. "Virginia called to say that Rose is refusing any more treatment. She wants us to call her hospital room in Omaha."

Rich and I stood in the back room of the nail salon, holding onto one another as we telephoned Rose. "There's nothing more to be done. The cancer has spread everywhere, and I'm trying to die today," Rose said, the tone of her voice deep with exhaustion.

Clasping my waist to steady my quivering stomach, I said, "I'm not sure, but I don't think it's something you have to *try* and do. I've heard you just have to let go." Looking back, I see how little I actually knew about it.

Rich took the phone to say his good-bye. He talked about the good times we'd had at the beach in Corpus Christi and, referring to the Title IX project we all did together, said, "We showed those coaches, didn't we, Rose?" With tears in his eyes, he said, "You will be with us always, Rose."

I loved him for being so present, so clear. I was anything but clear. I felt unsure of what to say, what to do. Mother was the nurse in our family, and Dad "didn't believe in sick." Rose and I were both "take two aspirins and keep on moving" kind of gals. Thinking there wasn't time for me to get to Nebraska for an in-person good-bye, I told her, "I'll get a plane out tonight and come be with your children." While on the plane to Nebraska, I scribbled some thoughts to help me process and prepare for what lay ahead:

> *Native Americans talk about how special it is to be with someone when they are "crossing over" from this life to the next. The expression "It's a good day for dying" comes from that attitude about death. Jyoti, a friend and midwife, says the time when life is coming in and the time when life is going out are the times that contain the most light, and it's the highest honor to be present on both of these occasions. I didn't get to witness my grandchildren come into the world, perhaps I will get to witness Rose's going out.*

At the time, I had heard an occasional person speak of the wonderment in witnessing a life coming in, and of course I'd experienced giving birth myself three times. But I'd known only one woman who told our women's spirituality group of the gifts she received in accompanying a friend through her dying process. I had to rely on this and the wisdom of indigenous cultures that know the truth of "a good day to die" to encourage myself to be with Rose. And since my son was living with a disease that would likely end his life before mine, at some level I knew that my assignment as his mother might include accompanying him on such a journey.

Now, seventeen years later, I hear people speak frequently of the miracle of witnessing a baby being born. Many people in our culture have taken back from the scientific/medical establishment the birthing process as a natural part of life. But in spite of the advances made by the hospice movement, there is still an overwhelming sound of silence regarding the wonderment of witnessing someone going out of this life. I suspect most people still have to call on the wisdom of ancestors when they take such a journey today.

>>> ▪ <<<

The late-night cab ride from the airport through intermittent rain showers offered a noir portrait of Omaha neighborhoods as the street-lights reflected in the wet pavement. I rolled my suitcase up the slick sidewalk into the University Medical Center lobby, down the long corridor to the wing and room that corresponded to the numbers on a crumpled slip of paper I was clutching. Entering the room, I was surprised to see Rose, wide awake, propped up with the help of pillows and the crank on the adjustable bed. An opaque white curtain hung from a metal rod dividing the room. But Rose had no roommate, and the many people in the room were all there to see her. Several Lincoln friends were there, having been recently joined by several friends who lived in Omaha. Hospital staff moved in and out, fidgeting with the shiny metal apparatus connected to the walls and the fluid-filled plastic bags connected to Rose.

We hugged one another enthusiastically, delighted that this meeting was able to happen. Rose seemed especially hyped up as she introduced me to her Omaha friends, some of whom had just learned of her impending death. This fact seemed to contradict the almost party-like atmosphere permeating the room and flowing out into the hallway.

After the friends and hospital staff members left and Rose and I were alone, she spoke softly, "Please stay with me as I do this, and I will be with you when it is your turn."

"Now, how could that be?" I thought, but I said, "I'll be here."

I'd always been astonished that Rose considered me her best friend. She was *my* best friend, but I didn't have as many friends as she did. She seemed to trust me in a way that she didn't trust other people. I felt honored and a bit scared by her request. It wasn't until much later that I came to realize the extent of this gift. The opportunity to accompany Rose as she let go of her life would provide lessons I was soon going to need in my own. Looking back, I think she was more aware of this than I was at the time.

As I'd left my house to go to the airport, I'd grabbed *Wherever You Go, There You Are* by Jon Kabat-Zinn, a book on mindfulness meditation that had come in the mail that day as a bonus for joining a book club. This chance incident would provide a valuable resource and navigational chart to help me come clearly into each present moment in Rose's hospital room. As Rose moved in and out of consciousness, it developed naturally that we meditated together. When we came back to "normal," or consensual reality, we would share our experiences. One afternoon, early in our time together, Rose's face became luminous.

"I figured out how to stop my cancer . . . I can show you."

She took a breath. "Now," she said.

After a pause and another breath, "Now," she repeated.

Having seen people in a hypnotic relaxed state, their eyes seeing inward in spite of being open, I knew that Rose was experiencing an altered state of heightened awareness and that something internal was actually happening to her.

"Now. Can you tell?"

"I see your face. You're beautiful!" I told her.

"The angels are helping me."

Later that day, Rose shared more about her experience. "Healing is breathing in the goddess," she told me, "and breathing out the disease. It takes place in the dark—from the darkness into the light."

I thought of my son Ken, who was living with AIDS. "I wish Ken knew about this."

"We can heal him. You're part of the miracle." Then she said a very singular thing. "When I leave, he will be clear."

Hope surged in my chest. I gasped, daring to engage the possibility that what Rose was predicting could come true. At the same time, my mind felt confused. I'd never been present when someone was dying. I had no intellectual understanding of what Rose was experiencing, no labels or ways to categorize it.

That evening, after Rose's son Mike had come to visit, I spoke with him in the hospital lounge. Mike was a practicing Buddhist, which may be why I felt drawn to tell him about this incident. I definitely felt the need to talk with someone about it.

He laughed and said proudly, "She's taking Ken's disease with her. She's a bodhisattva."

Excitement fluttered in my chest. "Bodhisattva—that's someone who postpones their own crossing to stay behind and help other suffering beings."

Mike nodded. With a touch of wonder in his voice, he said, "Mom is going through all the stages the scriptures talk about, and she hasn't even read them." He said that Rose was creating an energy field or body to go to "a place where there is no cancer."

As I hugged Mike good-bye, I felt awed by what I was learning about this journey into another dimension, a journey that he was naming and I was witnessing as I accompanied Rose.

>>> ■ <<<

The following morning, when I came into her room, Rose was in a dramatically different mood. "I'm sorry for getting you involved in all that *miracle* business," she said. "I think I was trying to see if there was a way that I could stay here." The tone of her voice told me she now realized that was no longer possible.

I recounted what Michael had said about her going through all the stages described in *The Tibetan Book of the Dead*, which neither she nor I had read. We had little information about the dying process and few rituals from our own culture to shepherd us through. We decided together that, like a lot of other tough things in life, we'd have to learn about it by going through it. I thought of what a Texas midwife friend had told me when she heard I was going to be with Rose. "This is your initiation into becoming a wise medicine woman." I'd told her how unprepared I felt, and she said, "If you weren't worthy, you wouldn't be there."

The word *mystery* came to me, and I took comfort in the idea that one little person like me doesn't know more than a thimbleful of what there is to know about life and death and everything in between. Rose and I would rely on one another, on the people who loved us, and on what Native American people call the Great Mystery to help us through this transformation.

>>> ■ <<<

On the fourth day in the hospital, Rose asked, "Seems like this is taking a lot longer than I thought it would. How does it seem to you?"

"It seemed that way to me too, but now I've come to think about it differently. That mentoring you did yesterday with that young intern— telling him not to trust the argument that there's no money for health care. I'm just waiting to see what other opportunities you'll have to pass on your wisdom before you get out of here."

After five days, one of Rose's doctors expressed a concern about Blue Cross's willingness to pay for the treatment she was receiving. "We aren't doing much for you, Rose, and there are facilities in Lincoln that have hospice services."

Rose became ferociously protective: she was determined not to die at home because of the distress and disruption it would cause her mentally challenged daughter. The house was Jolie's now, and she would not be able to understand what was happening to her mother.

"Call the governor. I hate to pull rank, but to hell with Blue Cross!" she said after the doctor left.

Friends did pull rank. A woman dressed in high heels and a suit from her meeting with the president of the medical center stopped by Rose's room. "I don't know if the governor got involved," she said, "but somebody important said, Leave her where she is." The hospital solved its problem by declaring her room a hospice room, and Blue Cross agreed to pay for services at that rate.

By the time we passed the one-week mark, my world had become Rose and the hospital room, her friends and daily visitors, hospital staff and cafeteria personnel. Beautiful autumn weather made journeys to the outdoor patio possible and pleasant, and the Omaha neighborhood burst with fall foliage during afternoon walks. At night, it was only a few steps across the street to my tiny dorm-like room and sleep. I stayed in contact by phone with three people: Rich, Corinne, who lived in Lincoln, and my friend and teacher Glenda, leader of our women's spirituality group in Texas, who became my coach and supporter as I supported Rose. "This phase of dying is referred to by Native Americans as ceremonial time," Glenda told me. "During this time, people move back and forth between the worlds—between this time and place and a place outside of time."

Thinking of the process in these terms helped me relate to the altered states that Rose and I and others traversed during those days and nights. Looking back now on this time of nearly total immersion, I'm struck by how much life there was in this process of dying. I remember it now as a blessed time, a time of deepest intimacy between Rose and me. There was only the present moment and little to do but to stay present in it.

>>> ■ <<<

When I arrived at 9:00 a.m. on the ninth day, Rose admitted that the video of nature scenes with music someone had set up hadn't helped her sleep. Rose's son David had visited the previous night to say his good-bye, but her daughter Jill still hadn't come. I had read that sometimes people wait to die until there is a completion with someone, and I thought this might be the piece that was holding Rose here. I called Jill, and David answered the phone. Jill was still sleeping. David told me he'd talked with Jill and told her how much better he'd felt after visiting their mother. Jill told him she'd think about coming.

Later, our mutual friend Maggie called Jill and reported back, "Jill wants to come tomorrow. She has meetings scheduled today, and she said she doesn't want people scheduling her life."

After Maggie left, Rose and I were meditating together, and Rose said she felt afraid. I told Rose, "I feel annoyed that Jill isn't coming today."

"Me too," Rose admitted. "Like she doesn't want to be inconvenienced."

I promised to call Jill again, and when I did, Jill said, "I guess I need to stop running away from this."

"I can only promise you will feel better coming than not coming."

Returning to the room, I told Rose what I sensed Jill was *not* saying and what she seemed to be avoiding. "Jill has a deep sorrow that you will not be there to help her raise her daughter."

"I know," she said, with deep sorrow in her own voice.

Then she began to get agitated. "I'm afraid to be in a bad place when Jill comes. I want to be able to give her love, but I'm not feeling that right now."

"You will. You were nervous about David yesterday, and it was a wonderful visit."

"Have I just been telling myself that I want to go, but really I'm not ready?" Rose asked. She had been clear about "trying to die" since she learned ten days earlier that her cancer had spread everywhere and that the situation was hopeless.

"Maybe it's like having a baby," I suggested. "We can be more than ready to be done with pregnancy, more than ready to become a mother, but our bodies don't always cooperate with our wills. My mother used to say, pregnancy is supposed to take nine months, but babies seem to come when they're good and ready. Perhaps something with Jill needs to get resolved. You may have something to teach your daughter before you go."

"Do you think I will be able to go once I talk to Jill?"

"Yes," I said, and I thought to myself, "*It's worth a try.*"

MEDICINE WOMEN

On the evening of the ninth day of my stay with Rose, I decided to drive to Lincoln to have dinner with my grandkids. For the entire sixty-minute drive west, I drove into an exquisite sunset. I never realized sunsets could last so long. Later, in my journal, I noted that like dying, each phase had its own beauty. Beginning as a glimmer, eventually the whole sky lit up; then there was just a glow on the horizon; and then an eerie light on the entire landscape as darkness fell. I wrote, *"The light doesn't cease, it just moves to another place, to be born again another day."*

On the afternoon of the tenth day, Rose's daughter Jill, dressed in a bright turquoise jacket over crisp blue jeans, all but waltzed into the room, gliding across to her mother's bedside.

"You look beautiful!" Rose said, and the love and pride she had for her daughter shone in her eyes.

"So do you, Mom," Jill said, with surprise in her voice.

"We've decided dying is a kind of beauty treatment," I told Jill. "Your skin smoothes out, and you even grow fingernails." I showed off my own longer fingernails as I tried to match their spirit of levity. I stayed with Jill and Rose for the first half hour of their visit, wanting to support both of them in this important time.

Rose told Jill she had seen a male figure in her room and she felt it was someone coming for her.

"What did he look like?" Jill asked. "Was he cute?"

"Now, would they send someone that wasn't cute? Of course he's cute," Rose said.

After Jill left, Rose said, "Do another ritual like you did this morning." I was taken aback because I'd thought she'd been asleep. That morning, I'd read a phrase in the meditation book, "Walking is stillness in motion, flowing mindfulness," and it had encouraged me to begin smooth, tai chi–like movements as a moving meditation in her hospital room. I knew that the movements would put me in a restful, centered place, and I hoped they would create a calm energy in the room.

When Rose asked for more ritual, I got out a tiny eagle feather, a gift from Glenda when Ken was diagnosed, and began moving with it, singing a chant I'd learned in the women's group: "Wearing my long-winged feathers as I fly . . . I circle the earth, the boundaries of the earth, the boundaries of the sky." As Rose drifted back to sleep, I said a prayer, "Great Spirit, take this woman to your bosom," and I felt the comfort of tears raining gently down my face.

>>> ▪ <<<

On the morning of the eleventh day, Rose asked me, "How's your time? Are you needing to get home?" I told Rose I'd spoken to Rich the night before. "He sounded tired but he told me he knew he was giving a gift to both of us by covering for me at the clinic and at home so I could be here. Rose then settled back restfully into her pillows.

When the nursing staff finished their morning routine, Rose and I descended into a meditative state, and I began singing to her another chant from the women's group. "I am woman. I grow out of the earth, beautiful, powerful, and wise." I showed her the dance that goes with it, and a smile of satisfaction came across her face.

"And I don't even understand the deeper significance of it," Rose whispered.

"At one level, it's about women feeling good about themselves and their connection to one another," I explained. "You can't do those movements and sing those words and continue to feel bad about yourself."

About this time, the nursing station received a call for me from Glenda, and though they'd never met, I decided to put Glenda and Rose on the phone with one another. Later, Rose shared some of their conversation. "Glenda mentioned she is preparing a talk for the Jung Society, 'Living Between the Worlds.' She told me the work we are doing is for the whole world. I told her this is women's work."

"I'm sure Glenda loved hearing that. She says that all the time. She says it's women's work to serve life in the coming in and the going out."

Women, and a few men, continued to come in and out of Rose's hospital room. They seemed drawn by the loving environment that surrounded Rose. It reminded me of the way family members gather around a young infant, marveling at the baby's tiny fingers and toes and every sound the baby makes. Time is made more precious because the infant will be with us only a short time before it grows and changes. Time with Rose became precious as we all recognized she would be leaving us soon. Some evenings, two or three women would gather with me around her bed and we'd sing. Rose, depending on her state of mind, would accept our serenade or gently laugh at our attempts to remember the verses to "Amazing Grace."

On the evening of the eleventh day, Rich broke down in tears over the phone and begged me to come home. Where the night before he had said he was okay with my staying, grief over losing Rose and the overload of maintaining the house and clinic was becoming overwhelming. But even hearing the pain in his voice, I knew I could not leave Rose.

>>> ■ <<<

By the twelfth day, two issues were emerging, likely on a collision course. Rose spent more time sleeping, and it became more difficult to awaken her for her oral pain medication, which needed to be taken every four hours. Her facial expressions and body language seemed to indicate that her pain wasn't as under control as it had been. Meanwhile, the hospital administrators began talking to us about moving Rose to a facility across the street, the Geriatric Rehabilitation Hospice Center. I wondered why they hadn't come up with this idea a week before. The surprised look on the doctor's face when he saw Rose after he'd been gone a couple of days suggested, in truth, that no one had thought she would last this long.

Rose appeared to be sleeping while the doctor discussed this new plan to move her, but after he left the room, she said to me, "Trouble is, I am fully coherent. I know everything that is going on."

I reassured her that I was on the watch, and if we needed to move across the street we would take our dancing and singing to the new space and it would be okay. But I prayed we would not have to move. The exhaustion I felt in my own body told me that this would be a tremendous task for everyone involved.

The following day, Rose's breathing changed. She began what one of the nurses called end-stage breathing. It looked like she was close to leaving until the nurses, with much effort, woke her to have her swallow her pain pill. This seemed stupid to me, though I didn't know what to do about it. In my mind, I called out to my deceased mother, "Dearest Jane, isn't there a better way?"

Four hours later, the nurses were unable to awaken Rose, so they skipped the pill. Soon afterward, her body language and facial expressions indicated she was in pain, and I began to feel very anxious. When the look on her face became like the face on Munch's painting *The Scream*, I confronted the medical team. With urgency in my voice I demanded, "Isn't there another way to manage her pain?" Someone on the team finally decided to double the medicine patches she was wearing, which didn't involve waking her. Annoyed, I thought, "Why has no one thought of this sooner?"

On the morning of the fourteenth day, as I hung up the phone with one of the women supporters I'd come to call the Comfort Sisters, I noticed Rose's noisy breathing get quiet. I walked over, sat beside her, and took her hand.

A nurse came in and said, "If she keeps breathing that way, she won't be here long."

She left the room, and another nurse came in. "I'll go and get the doctor. He's just down the hall."

I was alone with Rose and I realized: This is it. I began singing, "You are woman, you grow out of the earth, beautiful, powerful, and wise." Singing the chorus the second time, the words transformed: "You are woman, you go *back* to the earth, beautiful, powerful, and wise." And in that moment, Rose stopped breathing.

A nurse came in and examined her. "I don't get a heartbeat."

A doctor came in and confirmed it. She was gone. I could still feel her blood circulating in her hand, which I was holding in mine. I started to cry with tears of relief and sorrow and gratitude that Rose's ordeal (and mine) was over. Then I drew a blank as to what to do next.

The hospital staff let me stay alone with Rose for a few minutes. The clinical nurse specialist came in and, referring to my role in pushing for more pain management, told me, "You were a great patient-advocate this morning," and she gave me a big hug.

The nurse offered to call people, but I told her I would call the family. I began calling phone numbers and getting answering machines. When I reached one of the Comfort Sisters to tell her that Rose had crossed with me holding her hand, she responded, "Are you dancing?"

"What a good thing to say. Thanks for reminding me that's what I should be doing instead of crying, or rather *while* I'm crying."

>>> ■ <<<

The journey with Rose took fourteen days, yet it felt the fullness of an entire lifetime.

The depth of intimacy between us made it easier to let go of Rose. The promise she made when she asked me to be with her in her dying, "and I will be with you when it is your turn," finally makes sense to me. My turn has not come yet, but in the years since, what we went through together has made her a significant part of my life. Whatever has happened to me since, I have always known what Rose would have to say about it.

Returning from Rose's funeral, I remembered a comment Corinne made. She had teased me about becoming a "medicine woman."

"You better be careful, Mom. You get good at this and you might get more of these to do."

LIFE UPON THE
WICKED STAGE

After the high drama of Ken's AIDS diagnosis and Rose's crossing, our lives settled into a new normal. The field of behavioral health care had been changing rapidly, and not in a good direction as far as the financial reimbursements for providers was concerned. Not only were the big companies paying us less, they were taking way longer to cut us our checks. So Rich and I were spending long hours seeing clients and directing our behavioral health clinic and taking turns forgoing a paycheck. Ken was back at work and fixing up his dream apartment. He told me he was sure that a cure for AIDS was just around the corner and that his job was to stay healthy so he would be around when it got here.

Living with AIDS was not the first difficult challenge in Ken's life. I remember one afternoon after school discovering a seven-year-old Ken squinting his eyes up close into the bathroom mirror. "Is something wrong with my eyes?"

"It's not your eyes," I explained. "It's the way your brain is translating what your eyes are seeing. Sometimes a *b* looks like a *d* to you, and a string of numbers can get mixed up in your brain."

He continued to look confused. "Most everybody has this when they're little," I reassured him, "but some people take more time to outgrow it."

But Ken didn't grow out of his difficulties. School experiences, such as being called on to read out loud, brought fear and frustration. And his teachers had few tools to help him. The first kid in his Nebraska school district to be tested and labeled learning disabled, he got plenty of practice "faking it till you make it." School personnel tried each new approach developed for children with his learning difficulties, but he continued to lag behind his peers until he stumbled onto his own solution.

Fortunately, Ken inherited the family show business gene. Children's theater and after-school acting classes gave our Kenny a place to shine. His first professional job came at age seven in a dance I choreographed for the public television station where George worked. At thirteen, his youthful, all-American-boy look landed him a TV commercial for the Boy Scouts of America and an agent. Through the agent he found out about a university continuing education course, Auditioning Skills for Actors. The course was not for kids, and I felt apprehensive when he showed me the flyer. I thought about the process an actor goes through, getting the script with only a few minutes to look it over and being expected to read the lines out loud with authentic voice inflections. In this class, the sight-reading exercises would be videotaped and played back for the teacher and students to critique. Difficult enough for an adult actor, but for my child, with his reading difficulties, the whole idea ignited my mother-worry. But since it was something he came up with, I decided to let him try it.

"It was hard at first, watching myself messing up on the readings," Ken told me later. "But I got better. I was the only kid in the class, so no one laughed at me, and the other actors were really encouraging."

The real surprise came six months later when we learned at a meeting with Ken's special education teachers that he had jumped four grade levels in reading since taking the ten-week acting course. When I asked how this was possible, the reading specialist said that they didn't know. "It seems there's an on/off switch in the brain that relates to reading, and Ken has discovered how to turn his on." She emphasized that the chances of that switch getting turned on go up when the child is motivated to read something of high interest to him.

>>> ■ <<<

And now staying alive had become of high interest to Ken. Since musical theater continued to be Ken's passion, he found ways to use music to keep his spirits up as he learned to live with AIDS. He listened carefully to lyrics, as one might memorize a poem, and he often passed along tapes of the songs he discovered as gifts to those he loved.

"Nothing's gonna harm you, not while I'm around," he sang to an admired older woman in his role as the young boy character in a college production of *Sweeney Todd*. And "Nothing's gonna harm you, not while I'm around," he sang to me through a tape of the song he gave me to play in my car. That was shortly after I'd gotten a call from Ken about a rash on his leg that was giving him some pain. He asked me to go to the doctor's office with him as he checked it out. We both knew that this could be Kaposi's sarcoma, or KS, a rare cancer on the skin that can develop in someone with an impaired immune system. My heart sank when he described the rash, but I didn't want to jump to that conclusion too quickly. I e-mailed Glenda to put Ken and me and the upcoming doctor's appointment on the electronic prayer web.

I picked Ken up at his apartment in Dallas. The neighborhood he lived in wasn't the best, but he loved his apartment: the story-and-a-half living room with a ceiling fan, the fireplace, and especially the outdoor balcony. My tour started on the balcony, where he was just finishing watering the flowers.

"Recognize these square flowerpots? They're the ones we found at the warehouse sale where we found my sofa."

Seeing our round oak kitchen table reminded me of the time when Ken first started living on his own. He got behind in his rent and the landlord locked him out of his apartment with that very same table locked inside. I noted the contrast between how mad I was then and how proud I felt of him now.

In the waiting room of his doctor's office, I thought about what I knew about KS. In the early days of the epidemic, it was referred to as gay men's cancer because that was the population where a cluster of cases was first discovered. KS became an early marker for identifying people with unaccounted-for suppressed immune systems, and then it became a marker for AIDS.

We were called back into the examining room, and Ken introduced me to his doctor, one of three infectious disease specialists following his case. Ken reminded the doctor of the first time they'd met at the Dallas Halloween Parade, a raucous costume party and street fair beloved by gay men and their friends.

"You probably don't recognize me as the person who was wearing the blue chiffon gown and fake diamond tiara," Ken said. After examining Ken's leg, the doctor pointed out the small dark lesions on his skin. "Most likely this is KS. We'll biopsy it to be sure, but that's what it looks like."

I found myself taking a deep breath and stifling an impulse to sigh that would most likely bring tears. Ken's eyes flashed with fear as he bit down on his bottom lip.

The doctor's calm, steady voice continued, "What we see on the surface can occur inside the body as well, but as long as it stays on the skin and doesn't involve internal organs, it isn't life threatening. The first treatment would be some radiation to the leg," he told Ken. "And of course, we will work on getting your viral load reduced so your immune system can help in the fight too. There's a new drug to try and a series of drugs in the pipeline designed to be used together, each interrupting the virus at a different point in its life cycle. That cocktail-type treatment is about a year away."

Ken's mood brightened as he heard this. He said with a smile on his face and determination in his voice, "I know you guys are gonna find a cure, and I'm gonna take *really* good care of myself so I can be here for that happy day."

"Sounds like a plan. We'll start you on the radiation and see how your leg responds. There is also a kind of chemotherapy treatment we might consider later on." He paused, looking directly at Ken's thick, reddish-brown hair. He quickly added, "It doesn't cause you to lose your hair."

Keeping his hair was a big deal to Ken. It wasn't just vanity. It was about keeping his HIV status a secret so he could keep his concierge job. "I can't look like a sick person," he told me, "like I'm being treated for a disease."

A few months later, a change in managers caused Ken to be assigned the early-morning shift at the hotel. The medicine he was taking made it really tough to get up and going in the morning, so he had chosen to work the later shifts. But the new manager wasn't giving him that choice. On the early schedule, he began arriving late to work, so he decided to give up his beautiful apartment and move closer to work to shorten his commute during rush hour. I tried to reassure him with the mantra we used at the clinic when things didn't work out as planned: "It's this or something better, Ken." But my strategy wasn't working very well, since Ken couldn't imagine an apartment better than the one he was giving up, especially one he could afford.

One day, a former social work student and friend, a specialist in working with people affected by AIDS, asked me, "And *why* is Ken still continuing to work? His HIV status would give him immediate Social Security disability."

"Because he wants to" was the only answer I could offer. "He's young, and he loves his work. He's not burnt out from some job he hates that's worn his spirit down." And yes, it was difficult for me to see him struggling in a game whose rules were inherently unfair. His medical condition qualified him legally for special status and accommodations, although the social reality of the time demanded that no one at work could know about his HIV status.

He moved to a temporary place closer to work, which was kind of a dump. He didn't provide a tour whenever I came to take him out for dinner. He continued to have trouble adjusting to the new medicine.

He had trouble getting to sleep and trouble waking up, so after a couple of months, he was let go from his job.

Initially, Ken was devastated. We talked about his moving home, which he definitely did not want to do. Then, my resilient son began looking at the situation like he did his theater career. He came by the house with a box of file folders and notebooks, asking for my help and the use of our computer and printer.

"I need to update my work résumé, like I do my theater one. I've started making lists of my network contacts," he said, spreading dozens of business cards out on the dining room table. "Remember that guy Les and I met in Houston who's with the Ritz-Carlton? He might know someone in Dallas."

Just as he maneuvered to get auditions for theater parts he wanted, he used networking strategies for his job search. In a fairly short time, he got a job at the American Airlines Conference and Training Center near the Dallas Airport. The facility was expanding its conference offerings, and the staff was thrilled to have someone with Ken's experience at high-end, four-star properties in the hospitality industry.

Quite quickly, he and I found the perfect apartment a couple of miles from his new workplace. Not only did the living room have a cathedral ceiling with a fan and a fireplace like his former one, but the balcony overlooked the eighth hole of the golf course where Rich played golf two or three times a week.

Ken settled into his new job and came to feel he was making a real contribution. He was able to bring his skills to the new place and help them to create a stronger culture of customer service. "The answer is yes," Ken would say. "Yes, sir. We'll take care of that for you right away."

Come fall, he and I attended another AIDS, Medicine & Miracles conference in Houston and learned that the organizers were having trouble finding a venue for the following year's conference. When Ken mentioned his workplace, the organizers thought it would be ideal to have the conference at a facility so close to Dallas/Fort Worth Airport. Ken encouraged the conference organizers to apply and promised to do what he could from the inside.

From what Ken related to me, the ensuing meetings at his work did not go well. Ken's anger and disgust came through as he told me of the discussions: "They're afraid if they host the conference they'll have too many *sick people* in their facility, and it will drive other business away." Ken was anxious to testify to the hotel management about his own experience of the conference—how our family had attended the one in San Francisco and how helpful it had been when we needed it. But he kept quiet. He decided to bide his time until the following year, knowing that by then, he'd have built stronger relationships at the conference center. As I saw him grappling with this dilemma, I thought about what he once said about himself in comparison to his athletic older brother, Kevin.

"Kevin acts tough on the outside, but he's soft on the inside."

"What about you?"

"I'm the opposite. I'm soft on the outside but tough on the inside."

>>> ■ <<<

The following Christmas season, Ken invited me to be his special guest at his company's office party. Ken's boss, a woman around my age, sought me out to say how fond she was of my son. In a kind of mother-to-mother reassuring voice, she said, "He's been looking a bit thin lately, so I've been insisting he take his breaks every evening and eat something substantial."

As part of the entertainment for the party, Ken was to sing. The song he selected was from *Oliver,* a show he had done in college. "Consider yourself at home, consider yourself one of the fam-i-ly," he sang as his boss sat down beside me. At the end of the performance, we both applauded enthusiastically. She leaned over and whispered, "Aren't you proud of him?"

What she did not know and what I could not share with her was that on that very day, Ken had undergone his first radiation treatment during his lunch hour.

"Yes," I said. "I can't even begin to tell you *how* proud."

TO HEALTH

The morning sun sparkled on gentle waves as Corinne, Bill, Rich, and I waded in the shallow Gulf waters. Dressed in shorts and summer tops, we were catching up with one another at our favorite family vacation spot, the beach at Corpus Christi.

The grandkids, Ethan (a skinny four-and-a-half-year-old) and Will (a slightly rounder two-and-a-half-year-old), bravely explored the surf in front of our path. Covered with sunscreen, which caused the sand to stick to their skin and swimming trunks, they ran back and forth carrying small plastic buckets—filling and dumping Gulf water into a hole they'd dug on the shore. The sound of their laughter and splashing water provided the background for a most amazing announcement.

"I'm pregnant," Corinne said with a shy smile and a sideward glance toward her husband. "With *two* babies," she added, catching us so off balance that Rich and I drenched all four of us as we stumbled in the waves to surround Corinne and Bill for an enthusiastic group hug.

Corinne and Bill had been cautious in letting anyone know about the upcoming event too early. Her first pregnancy had miscarried after ten weeks, and even though she now had two healthy sons, it seemed wise to proceed with caution. But since they were about to tell the boys, keeping a secret wouldn't be an option much longer. After walking back to our small condo, Corinne showed us the sonogram.

"I need to get my glasses," I said, "because the image doesn't look right with two figures."

"It appears like they are in one sack," Corinne said, "but even the nurse couldn't be sure. If it is one sack, they're identical, and that makes them somewhat higher risk, and the pregnancy would be managed differently."

George arrived the next day after an eight-hour drive from Dallas, where he picked up Ken. George, retired from his work as a news broadcaster, traveled the country in his RV. His usual route went through Dallas, then to a campground in Nebraska near Corinne and her family, and then to Los Angeles, where Kevin lived. Despite our being divorced for more than twenty years, George often joined our family vacations, a practice that began when the older kids were in college and had only brief school vacations to get together with family. It probably also sprang from my determination as a family therapist. I became rather insistent with George that since we couldn't make a good marriage, we could work toward making a good divorce. I was grateful to Rich for his openness to this unusual arrangement and for his lighthearted references to George as his husband-in-law.

Ken couldn't go in the water because of the KS on his leg, but he walked along the beach and sat by the condo pool, cheering on his nephews in their brave attempts to swim away from the security of the pool's edge. Our middle child, Kevin, was the only one missing from the mix. The movie he was working on in LA was still in production and required his services. Kevin often missed our gatherings of late; either he was working and couldn't get off or he was not working and felt he needed to be actively looking for work. "I talked to Kevin last night," Ken told me, "and he mentioned he was mad at you. I told him, 'I support you to deal with these issues directly with Mom.'"

This information was not a surprise. Kevin had been "the angry young man" for about as long as I'd known him. He came into the world with an insatiable appetite, not addressed very effectively by me as I tried in the first few weeks of his life to breast-feed him while enduring a series of excruciating toothaches. So since our relationship's inception, there'd always been an edge of fierceness in our mutual devotion.

I did miss his being with us on family vacations, and I understood why he couldn't come when he had a job. And when he wasn't working but still said he couldn't come, I tried to remember how, having been in the theater myself, looking for your next job is never far away from your top priority, especially when you don't currently have one.

Seated at a table in our favorite seafood restaurant under the causeway bridge, Corinne told George and Ken her good news. The sonogram pictures passed back and forth across the red-checkered-oilcloth-covered table while Corinne looked on, her face luminous. "I'll go back in three weeks, and they'll look again to determine if the twins are identical."

The next morning, when Corinne and I went for a walk on the beach by ourselves, she mentioned offhandedly that she had found a tiny lump in her right breast the prior week. She'd visited with her doctor about it, and he suggested it was probably just a cyst related to the extra estrogen from the pregnancy. When I tried to suggest she might want to go further in checking it out, just for her own peace of mind, she became quite adamant. "It doesn't matter what it is, because we aren't going to do anything about it until I deliver."

I understood this remark was related to her belief that abortion, under any circumstances, was murder. She had refused amniocentesis with her other pregnancies because she would not terminate a pregnancy no matter what irregularities were discovered. I didn't completely share her view, but I realized that in my era, life had been different. Then, there were only a few inexact ways to track the condition of a fetus. Plus, abortion was still illegal. I respected her decision, but I did feel uneasy. She reassured me by reminding me of what her doctor had declared when they discussed the lump: "You have no risk factors for breast cancer."

After returning from our vacation, I placed our family and Corinne's twins on the prayer web of our women's circle. A few days later, Carol arranged a pipe ceremony for us in Fort Worth.

"Great Spirit, Great All That Is! Hear our voices. We come in a sacred way." Taking a small pinch of tobacco in her hand, the pipe carrier said, as she had done at the ceremony when Ken was first diagnosed, "I place in this pipe Grandmother Earth and Grandfather Sky." With each mentioning, she placed a pinch of tobacco in the pipe. "I place the two-leggeds, the four-leggeds, the no-leggeds, the winged ones, the plants and trees, the weather people, the mineral people. I place All My Relations in this pipe."

As the pipe was passed, each woman drew some smoke into her body and exhaled it into the four directions. The smoke of the sacred tobacco floated upward, and I felt the support and peace that comes from being connected to All That Is.

>>> ■ <<<

Returning from our vacation turned out to be, for many of us family members, a time for checking in with our health care teams. Ken needed to visit his doctor to set up his first chemotherapy treatment for the KS on his leg. I needed to visit my doctor to determine what was involved in a recommended surgery to repair a bladder condition that I had inherited from my mother and that had been exacerbated by my three pregnancies. And Corinne was to visit her doctor to find out if the twins were identical.

Ken's doctor postponed his chemo treatment until the following week since it was right before the July 4 holiday. "I want all the resources available the first time you have it." I took this to mean that some parts of the health care system shut down over the holidays or were staffed by a less experienced crew. And when I called to order the visualization tape Ken had used the previous year during his radiation treatments and had misplaced, the recorded message at the Body-Mind Medicine office declared the office closed for the week due to the Fourth of July holiday.

>>> ■ <<<

My journal entry on July 25 began simply: "Corinne's babies are dead." Corinne had called to tell me this news after she came back from what was supposed to be a routine doctor's appointment.

"During the scan to look for a membrane in between the twins, the nurse couldn't find the heartbeats," Corinne said.

"What does that mean?" I asked, struggling to comprehend what Corinne was saying.

"They were the right size for twelve and a half weeks," she said. "The membrane was there, so they were not identical, not high risk . . . but they weren't moving. Then the nurse saw some evidence of atrophy and determined . . . they were dead."

No warning signs, no symptoms. "Out of the blue," they call it. Like storm clouds rolling across a sunny sky.

"They did seem quieter the last day or so," Corinne said, "but that had happened before."

There was no miscarriage, no spontaneous abortion. The twins were still in her womb, which had become their tomb. I longed to pull Corinne close to me, to soothe her hurt, to spare her the pain I felt settling inside my own belly.

After Corinne's first pregnancy miscarried, she had come to Texas "to be with my mother," she'd said. Her doctor had told her that, in his experience, women and men look at this type of loss quite differently. "For men, the baby is a future possibility, and their loss is of their *anticipation* of a baby. For women, as soon as they know they're pregnant, the baby is a baby to them, and their loss is the loss of a child."

This sounded right to me, and I looked for ways to encourage her, even though our experiences were so different. Unlike me, Corinne's central goal in life was to have children and raise them. She had waited till after completing physical therapy school to begin trying to have children at age twenty-eight. I had been a somewhat reluctant mother, becoming pregnant at twenty-two, only six weeks after my wedding. I felt her deep sorrow and her worry that perhaps she wouldn't be able to have children. I'd never had a miscarriage, but I told her that my mother, her grandmother, had. It must have encouraged Corinne to learn that my mother had had eight pregnancies resulting in six living children, because after we talked about that, her mood lightened and we went shopping together for makeup and to have our nails done.

Now Corinne said matter-of-factly, "They'll do a D & C tomorrow since I haven't gone into labor." For me, the only silver lining was that now they would check out the lump in her breast.

After hanging up the phone, I thought of the pipe ceremony the previous Sunday afternoon. When it was my turn, I'd spoken honestly of my wish to have a granddaughter: "Since Corinne's announcement about the twins, I've been picturing myself with *two* granddaughters. It feels like I shouldn't admit this out loud because people always say, 'All that matters is that our babies are healthy.' But if they're identical, there is only one chance—two girls or none."

And now we knew—it would be none.

>>> ▨ <<<

In a second phone conversation that evening, Corinne described her experience of telling her son Ethan about the death of the twins. "He seemed confused when I told him, but later he came back, stood by me, and said, 'I want the babies to come out now.' I started to cry, and seeing me crying, he began to cry too."

I was awed at my daughter's wisdom as she told me how she comforted him: "It is very sad. There are lots of sad times and lots of happy times. But the sad times are shorter and the happy times are longer." She reported that a few minutes later, Ethan came back with a smile on his face: "See, Mommy, I'm happy now."

To comfort myself and help me accept this new reality, I wrote in my journal: "*We have no right to expect life to give us twins or to **not** give us twins.*"

I added a line I remembered from my Catholic-school upbringing. It was the mantra the biblical character Job used when faced with

TO HEALTH

multiple misfortunes: "*The Lord gives and the Lord takes away—Blessed be the name of the Lord.*"

Reading what I had written after this loss, I realize this expression is a way of saying, "I accept life on life's terms." And like all deep and abiding truths, it's way easier to say than to do. I have gone into and out of this acceptance, and I am still practicing it all these years since.

SPRING SHADOWS

I'd been hearing about Sedona for years. Its red rock formations, sculpted canyons, and sunsets were legendary, as well as its reputation as one of a few powerful "energy vortexes" on the planet. So, for a family vacation in early March 1997, we traded our Mexican time-share to go there. Ken very much wanted to come, but he was experiencing a great deal of fatigue from a new medication he was taking, so he asked for my help with packing.

One Saturday morning, Rich and I were greeted at the door of his apartment by a sleepy-eyed Ken, wrapped in his favorite purple comforter, its fringe trailing on the floor behind him. Clothes were piled everywhere, in his bedroom and on the floor of his closet, while dirty dishes and food packages overflowed the sink and countertops. His sense of pride in having his own apartment and his usual artistic decorating sense had been overridden by his need to rest between work shifts. As we took clothes from the dryer, Ken sat on his blue denim sofa folding the laundry we brought to him. He told us he wouldn't be able to travel with us because of his work schedule, but he'd follow behind a few days later. I didn't like this plan, but I knew better than to try and talk him out of it.

When George and Kevin went to the airport in Arizona to pick Ken up, they didn't recognize him. Kevin returned to the condo and said, in a voice of some urgency, "We need to have a family meeting to talk about how we can support Ken." Looking back, Rich and I had probably gotten used to Ken's decreased energy state and emaciated look. Kevin and George's experience was a kind of wake-up call.

We had the family meeting, which was a practice left over from when the kids were teenagers and one of us (usually a parent) would call a meeting to iron out some difficulties with schedules or chores. In those days, it was common for someone (usually a kid) to balk at having to attend, and this time Corinne was the reluctant participant. Before we sat down at the long conference table in the main lodge, she confronted Kevin. "This is our vacation. I was hoping to have some time alone with my husband while the grandparents are here to watch the boys. I resent your flying in from California with your dramatic 'big brother' concern for Ken."

Kevin didn't back down. He insisted that Ken needed our help. He wanted Ken to have a chance to let us know how we could help him. As though brainstorming ideas with colleagues at a film production meeting, Kevin suggested a nutritionist he knew in California. He was sure this man could help Ken gain some weight and regain his energy. Ken responded with openness to this idea, and I felt proud that Kevin was so dedicated to helping Ken. But as the meeting continued, my eyes were drawn to the large windows and the scene beyond of gigantic rust-colored boulders against a sun-streaked purplish sky. Like Corinne, I wished in that moment that we could be out there rather than inside grappling with such tough issues.

Ken demonstrated the truth of Kevin's concern by rarely getting off the condo sofa for the rest of the week.

Throughout the three years since Ken's AIDS diagnosis, there had been occasions when various treatment trials and their side effects left him with little energy. I had been hoping this was just another one of those periods. But it was becoming clear to us all that something was terribly wrong. We visited the Chapel of the Holy Cross, built between two red rocks on a so-called vortex spot. A wide-angled window behind its altar offered an excellent view of jagged rock formations and sun and shadows dancing on their surfaces. It took me into another dimension. As I knelt at the communion railing to say a prayer for my son and our family, a feeling of nearly overwhelming sorrow rose up from my chest and on to my face. Tears began forming in the corners of my eyes. As the mother in this scenario, I'd tried to stay in a positive and hopeful place about Ken. He himself was confident a cure would be found and I often heard his mantra, "My job is to take very good care of myself so I will be here when the cure comes." My tears betrayed my fear that his dream might not be realized.

On the plane returning to Dallas, Ken admitted to me that he hadn't been taking his Bactrim. He confessed that the desensitization process he had undergone to be able to take it had only lasted a short while, and then he was back having the uncomfortable hive-like symptoms. So he'd stopped taking the drug. And he didn't tell anyone, including his doctors.

I felt a rage boiling inside me at this revelation. As we drove directly to the hospital from the airport, I stayed silent. I didn't want my anger to explode all over this sick kid, but I was convinced that this explained what was wrong with him. In my mind I thought, "He has pneumonia, one of the ways that people with AIDS die, and it is preventable."

>>> ■ <<<

"I'm relieved it isn't PCP pneumonia," I told Rich as we drove home from the hospital after Ken was admitted. "But with all the tests they're running, if there is anything else going on in his body, they will find it." I noticed that instead of feeling encouraged by this thought, I felt a strong sense of dread.

In the following few weeks, driving back and forth a couple of times a day between the hospital in Dallas, our home in Arlington, and our clinic in Fort Worth, we got into a routine. George was with Ken in the mornings, I visited in the afternoons, and Richard would come in the evenings. We conferred daily with his doctors, who had established that he didn't have pneumonia, but they didn't know what he did have.

As his doctors and we family members searched the medical research files available on the Internet in the family reception area, Ken was to continue taking the many pills that made up the newly discovered AIDS "cocktail," a strategy that looked hopeful but was unproven at the time. The doctor had said, "Let's keep the level of the virus down while we figure out what else might be going on."

One particularly beautiful sunny Sunday morning, I decided to get a wheelchair and take Ken outdoors for a brief ride around the hospital grounds. He had seemed depressed, and I thought some fresh spring air might lift his spirits. Before we started our outing, he went to use the restroom and I began straightening his bed linens. A fluffy white stuffed bear, given to him by his sister and her two sons, sat propped up in the middle of the bed pillows. Around the animal's neck was a multicolored, hand-woven medicine pouch, a Native American ceremonial item given to me by one of the women in my spirituality group. I don't remember how it got fastened around the bear's neck, but as I moved the animal, pills begin spilling out of the pouch. Pulling back the covers, more pills rolled out of the bed sheets and onto the floor. I knew immediately that the pills were Ken's HIV medication, the cocktail that we all (especially George) had been trying to get into him. When I showed the pills to George, he put his hand to his head and shook it in disbelief. "I might just as well leave. There's no reason for me to be here," he said with anger and disappointment in his voice.

I felt my face flush and the back of my neck stiffen as I struggled to face the truth. I thought about how I believed that facing the truth, however painful or inconvenient, was always better than avoiding reality. Wheeling Ken outside to a park-like area near the hospital, I had to admit that my son did not subscribe to that same principle. George, who wasn't good at confrontation, excused himself to go find a nearby railroad museum he'd read about.

The moment the pills spilled onto the floor, I knew that Ken was going to die. I would go in and out of that realization, but I could no longer hold on to the hope that medicine could keep him alive. Before that time, and many more years since, there were stories of people with AIDS being near death but recovering to live well with the disease. But all that hinged on getting the viral load down and keeping it down so that the person's own immune system could fight off whatever was threatening his life. It seemed to me that Ken knew this and he was not taking the actions needed to stay alive. Did he want to die? Was he worn out from fighting to stay alive?

I prayed silently before kneeling down beside Ken's wheelchair. I said, "Ken, I found the pills you stashed in the teddy bear's pouch. We need to talk about your death."

I reminded him that I had helped Rose die and I would help him if that's what he wanted, if he didn't want to go on with treatment anymore.

Ken began to cry. "I don't want to die. I want to live and be here with you all."

It felt good to hear that, but I wasn't sure he meant it. "It's okay if you're ready to leave. You've been through so much. We can talk about your funeral, your will, what you want to happen with your things."

Then he got angry. His face began to flush. "I have been doing so good on walking and *trying* to do good on eating."

"It seems like you're giving mixed messages. What I want . . . remember what I said when we found out you had AIDS? As awful as the news was, it felt good getting my son back. I want us to have as much honesty and truthfulness as we can, no lies or hiding."

He agreed. Then he moved into a problem-solving mode. "It's easier for me to take my pills when the nurses give them to me and stand there while I take them."

"Ken, the nurses can't give you those pills because they're part of a drug trial. They're not from the hospital pharmacy. It's a legal thing with their license. That's why your father has had to give them to you. He's taken the pills on as his job, and he's done the best he could in getting you to take them. You need to make amends to him about this."

When Ken's doctor found out about the medication, he shook his head gently. "Ken has always seemed to have a healthy dose of denial, which has served him well. But now it's working against him," he told me, and I agreed.

All the while, Ken's health was taking a turn for the worse, and during his hospitalization, there was another area of extreme stress going on in our lives. Coming up on the tenth anniversary of our clinic, we were in negotiations to sell it. The health care environment had become more and more difficult for providers, especially in behavioral health. Rich and I had tried working harder and longer, expanding with more locations and employees, then downsizing, reducing back to one campus. After a period of taking turns taking a salary, we decided it was time to consider an offer to be purchased. I especially didn't want to do it; the clinic was like another of my children, but Rich said we couldn't keep going as we were. And InterPlay friends Cynthia and Phil advised, "Don't feel bad. You've done everything right. It just isn't working."

So in the middle of the heartbreak of Ken's illness, we had to learn about mergers and acquisitions, stocks and buyouts, non-compete clauses, and employment agreements. Ours would not be one of those situations where people sell their business and retire on the money they make. Being purchased for us meant we wouldn't have to close the clinic and we wouldn't be taking that debt with us to continue paying off into and past our retirements. To avoid complete overload, I left the details of the acquisition to Rich and kept my focus on my son and anything I could do to support him.

Medical detectives continued their work on Ken's case diligently. As at a crime scene, they collected and compared evidence from his body to a national database, looking for a match of DNA or blood types, or in this case cell signatures. They took fluid from Ken's lung and found lymphatic cancer cells. They weren't expecting this, so they had to analyze it further. The oncologist planned to contact physician friends in San Francisco to see if there was anything new on this disease that hadn't been published yet.

Ken's regular doctor asked him, "Do you want me to treat this aggressively?"

"Yes. I'm not afraid of chemotherapy. I've had it before."

"This is a stronger treatment; your hair will most likely fall out."

After the doctor left, Ken told me, "I don't think my hair will fall out. I have really good hair."

I didn't argue with his belief. I just accepted it as another instance of how Ken's childlike, innocent ways were still protecting him from the harshness of reality.

>>> ■ <<<

Ken's cells marked as T cell lymphoma, which the doctors said was impossible. He couldn't have T cell lymphoma because he had HIV. That type of cancer is a slow-growing skin cancer. Meanwhile, Ken took chemo slowly over a four-day period because of his compromised condition. He survived it, but the KS on his leg swelled and started to give him pain. His white cells went to zero, and he was fed intravenously at night to build him up. He didn't have enough protein in his system, so his body retained fluids—enough fluid that his weight went from 145 to 190. Dr. Allen referred to him as a beached whale. Ken handled this "joke" better than I did. It was too close to the truth.

During this whole period, I felt like I was running up a steep hill that twisted and turned, changing directions as soon as I got into any kind of a manageable pace or rhythm. I decided to turn my attention away from the medical detective story and focus on Ken's thirty-first birthday, which came on the first of April.

In his best professional hotel concierge voice, Ken gave me directions for his celebration: "Go to Eatzy's (a gourmet grocery store where patrons shop to the accompaniment of opera arias) and pick up dinner. Bring a tablecloth for my tray table and we'll all eat together."

Les bought the cake and helped with the shopping, keeping everything refrigerated at his apartment until we were ready for it. Kevin flew in from California to help celebrate. Rich, Kevin, and I commiserated with one another and admitted how discouraged we were about Ken. He'd been in a lot of pain, and the medication kept him in and out of being a participant at his own party. By Sunday we were doing better emotionally, but Ken was not.

Rich initiated a "talent show" event in Ken's hospital room. He brought hair clippers, and hairdresser Les demonstrated his skill and then supervised me while I cut Richard's hair. George told stories about the Oregon lighthouse where he volunteered. Though we'd heard most of the stories before, we enjoyed the retelling. Kevin told stories of his two dogs, how he found them, or rather how they found him, and how he nursed them back to health. As I got up to go to the restroom, Rich teasingly announced, "Sheila's going to get her tap shoes and change into her costume for a dance number."

>>> ■ <<<

While Ken's hospital life involved full-time lying in bed, he often played music from his extensive collection of musical theater scores. One afternoon I offered to massage his leg, which was painfully swollen and itching. After I donned latex gloves and began a gentle massage, I became aware of a song from the movie version of *The Sound of Music* playing in the background: "For here you are, standing there, loving me, whether or not you should." The words of the song became foreground as I continued the rhythmic motions. It became a kind of blessing: "Nothing comes from nothing, nothing ever could, so somewhere in my youth or childhood, I must have done something good." Tears came to Ken's and my eyes, and to Rich's as he observed from a chair in the corner of the room. "Here you are standing there loving me," the soothing words and melody repeated, and we all realized some force of nature, bigger than us, had arranged that synchronicity. "I must have done something good"—an elegant confirmation that Ken and I and Rich were lovable and deeply loved.

Meanwhile, my friends who were practitioners in alternative and complementary medicine got involved. My friend Jyoti, a former midwife, put me in touch with a naturopath friend in New Hampshire. After a conference call with her, I went to the health food store for liver herbs and tea, and she mailed me some nutritional supplements for Ken. With these supplies, and a Juiceman Junior, we started juicing in Ken's room, which made Kevin happy since he saw nutrition as the best medicine. In a few days, Ken's white cells came back, and the doctors felt he was strong enough to take Taxol, a drug that had a good record with KS. He took it well, and it began to make a difference in his leg.

Next problem: Ken had been on his back for a month and had lost a great deal of strength and flexibility in his body. The doctors ordered physical therapy, and when the therapist arrived, she commented, "I wish they'd called me sooner." The doctor decided to move Ken to a rehab floor after realizing that, to go home, he would need more mobility. The rehab doctor took an army sergeant approach. "It's time to fish or cut bait. If you want to live, you have to get out of bed!"

This attitude, and the physical therapist, helped Ken. He graduated to a potty chair, then wheelchair, then walker. George identified the pain medication as the biggest threat to Ken's recovery because when he took it, he got nauseous and couldn't eat. George knew of a wristband people wear on ships that touches a specific pressure point and prevents motion sickness. I picked one up at the drugstore and brought it with me to the hospital, along with more of Ken's music.

Just when things seemed to be looking up there was another, freakish development. For the investigators of this who-done-it assault on Ken's health, there was a break in the case. Ken woke up one morning with a spongy, finger-shaped tentacle protruding upward about a half inch from the top of his left shoulder.

"Looks like, whatever this is, it's sticking its tongue out at us," the doctor said. "But at least now we have something to biopsy."

The lab report from the biopsy came back with cells that didn't match any known disease. The scientists began sharing this information internationally through the Internet. In twenty-four hours they'd found four other cases in the world that matched Ken's cells, all HIV/AIDS patients. The diagnosis was a rare form of an aggressive immunoblastic lymphoma, whose cells had mutated to get around the host's severely impaired immune system.

The oncologist came to talk with Ken about his options. He spoke mostly to me, for Ken to overhear, which I found annoying. He began with a long spiel about living wills and do-not-resuscitate directives and then he said, "It's not likely that chemotherapy would work for Ken. The traditional treatment for lymphoma would kill him." He recommended a drug that would help the KS. "I see that as a greater threat than the lymphoma in the short run."

The next day, Rich and I drove over to Dallas to meet with Ken's regular doctor, the one I had talked with on the phone when Ken was first diagnosed. We had lots of questions for him. What if Ken doesn't get treatment? How long would he have?

Dr. Allen came into the hospital room and sat on the foot of Ken's bed. He looked at Ken directly and spoke to him with tenderness in his voice. As I viewed this surreal scene from the other side of the bed, the two men looked like soldiers in a MASH unit, the older an officer in charge of the other. And now, after their battlefield experiences have come to an end, the officer tenderly communicates to the younger one that he will not survive his injuries.

"This type of lymphoma is mean and fast-growing; that's why it's called *blastic*. There's no cure. You could do chemotherapy, but it isn't gonna change the outcome. If you don't do treatment, you have a month or two. If I were you, Ken, and it's important to say that I'm not you. But if it were me, I'd go home, get my affairs in order, and enjoy whatever time I have left with my friends and family."

Ken immediately argued, "I don't want to give up. I feel it's important to do *something.*"

"It's your decision. We can arrange for the chemotherapy, which may be able to control some symptoms and keep you comfortable."

I asked the doctor why he wouldn't try chemotherapy if he were in Ken's place. He said, "With this type of lymphoma, you're likely to get relapses. You're in and out of the hospital, and it's questionable whether you'd get any time of real functioning or quality of life." He disagreed with the other doctor and insisted that KS was not the biggest concern. The nutrition picture was, and we could help that by changing the antibiotic and getting some anti-nausea medication so Ken would be able to eat. He recommended medical marijuana in pill form. "You take it thirty minutes before eating."

I later told Dr. Allen that some of my women friends were healers and that they wanted to come see Ken. He didn't ask any questions about what they would do when they came. He just said, "We can wait until tomorrow afternoon to start the chemo, so your women healer friends can see him in the morning."

I'm not sure whose idea it was at first, but my friend Lu, a Sufi healer, took charge of the group of healers. Lu did various types of bodywork, some of which she had learned working with a chiropractor and some growing up in the South in an African American community. She had invited a nurse member of her Sufi community to join us. Jyoti, also a nurse, brought her experience with chanting meditation and sound healing. Her friend Feizi, the naturopathic physician I had consulted by phone, was in town and came along. I was the fifth member of the group. The naturopath examined the paperwork on Ken's blood counts, and the numbers for his liver enzymes alarmed her. She made plans to talk with Ken after we finished so he would understand what he needed to do to protect his liver from more damage from the drugs they were giving him. She suggested we not bring heat to our hands when working with Ken but light and cool energy.

Lu set the parameters for our work together. She directed us each to take a specific part of Ken's body and direct energy to that part. "The session would take about an hour. It will have a life of its own and we will know when it is finished."

The women stationed themselves around Ken as he lay in his bed,

Jyoti at his feet, Feizi at his head, Lu on his right, me on his left. The nurse from the Sufi community stationed herself at the door, making sure that nothing interrupted the energy field that we would be creating. In a tone of "it's no big deal," Lu told Ken, "You might have an emotional response to the work we're going to do. So you know, crying is fine. Screaming is fine. Just tell us. We'll give you a pillow if you need to cry into it."

Ken smiled and relaxed into the process. Everyone, including Ken, went into a trance, and I'm sure each of us had our own unique experiences. I got memories of being with Rose when she described the experience of "stopping her cancer." I had always felt that she was on to something, but neither of us knew how to take advantage of her discovery. I remembered the unusual rhythm of her breath in that experience, and I picked it up in my body as I moved the energy around Ken's chest and heart area. Another memory came to me of being in labor with Ken. I wrote in my journal later:

> *Instead of the trunk of my body working to turn Ken so he could be born as a baby into this life, this time my hands are moving to re-form him, so he can go through the next birth canal to his new life—on this plane or the next one.*

Ken didn't appear to have a reaction to the work until that evening, when he was dozing off while receiving his chemotherapy. He told George, who was with him, "This is the worst. I'm having terrible nightmares." When I heard about it, I offered to come by or to get a therapist to come.

"I'd rather have someone else come. Someone not so closely involved."

So I sent a former social work student of mine who had experience working with AIDS patients and who knew Ken. I was careful not to ask any questions of her or of Ken, but he seemed much better emotionally after he met with her.

Now, years later, I see the healing ceremony that my women healer friends and I did as a way of sending light and love to Ken. All medicine sends messages to the cells to change their behavior (reduce inflammation, halt reproduction), and our messages to Ken were, "We care about you, and because healing takes place from inside, we join our individual healing energies and offer them to your body/mind system to do for you whatever it is that you need." I'm certain there was an outcome for Ken from our work, though I do not know the particulars of what it was. There may have been an emotional wound that got healed, particularly after he had a chance to process whatever came up with his therapist. As we must do throughout our lives, we offered our gifts and let go of the outcome because that is not for us to determine.

I took my cues from Ken because, like his doctor, I was aware that this wasn't about me, or what I would do in his situation. I put on my social worker hat and began making plans for Ken to come to our home and to close up his apartment. Ken insisted that his furniture be put in storage near the apartment so he could move back there easily when he got stronger. I didn't think that was at all likely, but I did what he requested.

THE DYING ROOM

The room was my favorite room in any house we'd ever lived in. The first time I walked into it, when the real estate agent showed us the house, the floor-to-ceiling stone fireplace caught my eye, then the dappled sunlight streaming in through large windows on either side of it. And high up near the two-story ceiling, smaller windows exposed tree limbs and foliage, bringing the forested outside into the cedar-paneled great room. I stood still and silent, drinking it all in. I didn't need to see the rest of the house. I knew instantly this was the one we'd been looking for.

Ken was a teenager at the time we'd bought that house, and he'd been with me through the five-year search through fifty houses before we found it. Looking for just the right house at the right price had been taking way too long for Rich. And since Ken enjoyed decorating and designing spaces as much as I did, he happily came along. Now, twelve years later, a rented hospital bed occupied the center of that room, and Ken was sleeping fitfully in it. Medical paraphernalia was stacked on the desk and credenza, and friends and family moved quietly between his bedside and the sunroom beyond. A woman from our circle brought food and flowers and lingered in the kitchen. "It's hard to leave; the energy of this place seems sacred, holy. You can feel the love in this place," she said as she hugged me good-bye.

We were keeping a vigil—watching, guarding, and praying. On Monday night we'd entered what Native Americans call ceremonial time, when the doctor had said we must "change our focus." We had moved from treating Ken to keeping him comfortable, and although doctors don't tell you this, our job now was to help him make his transition. I called Corinne in Nebraska, who a few months after losing the twins had become pregnant and was now in her seventh month. I suggested she come as soon as possible instead of waiting for the weekend to come with her husband and kids as planned. I worried she wouldn't make it in time, even though part of me knew everything would work out exactly as it should.

George had his RV parked in our driveway. He'd been in town from Oregon for three months, taking shifts with Richard and me. This family caregiving team and routine had been put in place when Ken had first been diagnosed with AIDS three and a half years before. We'd reactivated it in March, when Ken was hospitalized in Dallas. George, a faithful father, had learned to give shots and was now keeping track of temperatures and medication regimens. The tough spot for him was the emotional part. Tough for all of us, but tough for George in particular. We had trouble convincing him it was time for us family members to talk with Ken about the "change in the focus."

"I don't think we need to put the boy through group therapy, Sheila."

This was a flashpoint between us that went back even before we married. I noticed remnants of resentment rising in me as we stood talking in the center of the kitchen. I took a couple of breaths and then surprised myself by saying in a quiet voice, "Ken's different from you, George. Remember, he *likes* group therapy."

But I backed off. I reminded myself that Ken understood and accepted this part of his father better than I did.

"You know Dad," he would joke, "Mr. Emotion."

Corinne arrived Thursday night. Kevin had been back and forth from California every couple of weeks and was now with Ken every night, sleeping on a sofa in the great room. It was after midnight and I was in bed, half-drifting into sleep, when I heard a gut-wrenching howl. The sound persisted in waves that reverberated throughout my entire body. I jumped out of bed, frantic. What could be happening?

Rushing into the great room, I saw Kevin attempting to put his arms around his younger brother to calm him. Ken was sitting up in bed, arms flailing, as he pulled away from Kevin and continued to howl.

We managed to get an anti-anxiety pill under Ken's tongue, which soon calmed him. Later, after Ken had fallen asleep, Kevin explained, "I couldn't lie to him. He kept asking me, 'What is going on? What is happening to me?' I finally told him straight out, 'You're approaching death.'"

Kevin had broken through the silence, the denial we had been allowing Ken to hold onto. With the pain of Ken's howl still ringing in my ears, I began questioning myself: Should I have told him? Should I have persisted in getting the family together to talk with him? No answers to my questions came. I thought about the people I knew who were praying for us, and for me in particular, and I imagined hearing them say, "Sheila, you are doing the very best you can." I went back to my room and lay down on the bed. I fell asleep to a message that became my mantra: "We are ALL doing the best we can."

Later that same night, Ken awoke crying out in a demanding voice, "I need more rope. Get me more rope." Kevin came to get me in my bedroom. Getting more frustrated by the moment, Ken repeated, in a loud voice, "I NEED MORE ROPE."

Remembering that people in his condition sometimes think in metaphorical, dreamlike language, I said, "Do you mean that you are at the *end* of your rope? That's why you need more rope?"

"YES," he said with a big exhale, relieved that we finally understood his meaning.

By the next day, Ken was sleeping a great deal of the time while family members, and occasionally one or two of Ken's friends, moved in and out of the nearby sunroom. My kid sister, Maureen, and her husband, Steve, had come in from the country north of Dallas where they lived. As I entered the sunroom, I was surprised to hear that the conversation had turned to a discussion about my *brother* Kenny, after whom my son was named.

No one had ever been arrested or charged with my brother's murder, and strangely, our family still knew very little of the details of his death. A few months after his disappearance, but fully a year before his body had been discovered, our parents had visited the rural county where he had been living. They'd found no answers, returning only with suspicious forebodings. My dad had confided to me privately, "I don't know what happened to Kenny, but he's not alive."

At Mother's pleadings, all five of us siblings had promised never to go to the county where he disappeared to conduct our own investigations. She could not bear to have another of her children come to harm, and she was convinced that would happen if we started poking around there. This afternoon, as the discussion on the sun porch continued, I learned for the first time that Steve had visited the area a year and a half after Kenny's death. "I know who killed Kenny and how it happened," Steve said. I looked at Maureen, wondering how long she had known this.

Not only was what he said shocking, but shocking also was that shy, quiet Steve had just spoken more words than I'd ever heard him say in the seventeen years he'd been a member of our family.

In the quiet room, Steve continued, "When I visited, the locals didn't realize I knew Kenny's sister, so they were open and up-front with me. Kenny had done construction work for some guy named Ollie. It involved laying a sidewalk, and Kenny was paid for the job. Apparently, he left part of the job unfinished because he had to go to California, but he promised to finish when he got back. Kenny's hippie friends said Ollie was upset about it and about some other thing involving money."

Steve said these friends claimed they were blackmailed into getting Kenny to come with them up into the forested mountain so that Ollie could "teach him a lesson." Steve said the friends expected someone might "rough him up a bit." But when Kenny bent over to check an animal trap, Ollie's nephew shot him in the back of the head.

Steve paused and then added in an exaggeration of his country twang, "These good ol' boys been marrying their cousins for a couple of generations, so they ain't too swift in the intelligence department. They threw the body over a cliff, where those hunters found it two seasons later."

Family members present remembered when the body was discovered, a year and a half after Kenny's disappearance; how dental records had confirmed his identity; the funeral; and the burial of his remains in the family plot in Kentucky. We recounted how our mother had joined him eight years later, having never recovered from the loss and the fact that her peace-loving son had died violently. I thought (but didn't say) that when I first learned that Ken had AIDS, I became afraid for myself, that I would follow in my mother's footsteps, not able to survive the death of my son. I wondered how far I'd come in my acceptance of my son's destiny.

After the others left, Kevin, Rich, and I talked, sitting in the room where Ken was sleeping. I realized that both my brother's and son's stories were Judas stories—both were betrayed or harmed by friends. My brother Kenny, who risked jail to become a conscientious objector, who did alternative service in a hospital during the Vietnam War, died at age twenty-six, apparently delivered up by friends to his executioner. My son Ken, when asked how he'd contracted AIDS, once gave the answer, "Low self-esteem." I never asked Ken when and where he thought he had become infected, but I imagine it was from someone he trusted.

While we talked, I noticed Rich twirling an owl feather between his fingers. I remembered it had been given to Ken by one of the women in my spirituality group. "The owl represents being able to see in the darkness," I said, "into the unknown."

Kevin said, "Hey, Uncle Kenny's Indian name was Moon Owl!" I'd forgotten that, and when he said it, I got chills down my arms. It felt as though the energy of my brother Kenny had just come into the room.

In my journal that evening I wrote,

So Spirit is here! The light is strong and it is working—healing many layers in all the people who are connected to this man-child. What he came to do—he is doing even now, as he lies on his deathbed.

I now know, having come through this, that healing often takes place in the group body of the family when a member is transitioning. These ceremonial times, as the native people speak of them, bring an increased light of awareness as the veil between the worlds is thinned and sometimes lifted.

>>> ■ <<<

When Corinne stood by Ken's bedside, I noticed he wasn't acknowledging her presence. True, he had grown unable to speak, but often he was aware and responsive to those around him. In her presence, he seemed to be shielding himself. I wondered if this had to do with her aversion to his being gay. Desperate with love and concern, Corinne had sent Ken many letters over the years, asking him not to live as a gay man because she was afraid he wouldn't be able to go to heaven.

A social worker friend advised me to bring this issue out in the open or it would continue to block Corinne and Ken's communication. I suggested to Corinne there might be a need to clear any sense of judgment or criticism with Ken.

"I felt I did that," she said, with tears in her eyes, "in the letter I wrote him after my visit to Dallas."

"Just remind him of what you wrote again—perhaps it will be said or heard differently now," I suggested.

So with Corinne present, I spoke to Ken about how much she loved him. "Corinne has had some difficulty with some of your choices and life decisions—but she truly loves you," I said, holding each of their hands while I spoke. Then I left them alone.

I don't know what Corinne said to her younger brother in private, but I was present when she left his side to go to bed. He was not expected to make it through that night, and she said her final good-bye in the most powerful way possible. She leaned over the head of his bed, putting her arms on his shoulders and laying her head on his pillow. She kissed him on his forehead and spoke softly into his ear. Referring to the twins she'd lost a year earlier in a miscarriage, I heard her whisper, "Take care of my babies."

In the room's dim light, I felt sure I saw a glimpse of recognition on Ken's face. I hugged Corinne and took a deep, grateful breath.

After everyone had gone to bed, I was alone with Ken for my shift. It was a few minutes before midnight on a Friday night and Kevin was asleep on the sofa on one side of the room. Memories of dancing flooded my mind—dancing in my friend Rose's hospital room as she lay dying, dancing at her funeral service, and dancing at the women's retreat at a ranch in North Texas with my women's spirituality group. I remembered that during one retreat, as I was dancing on behalf of Ken, out of the corner of my eye I caught sight of a framed picture of him, sitting on the altar beside a dozen or so other pictures of group members' families. Without stopping the dance, I scooped up the picture and, clutching it to my chest, continued dancing with it as the Glide Memorial Church vocalist sang, "I haven't always been as good as I can be, but God is good to me." Lu, a practicing Sufi, told me later, "You've just demonstrated my religion. Whatever it is that life hands us, we pick it up and dance with it."

These memories encouraged me to dance there, in that moment, in Ken's dying room. My dance was slow, a tai chi type of moving meditation, emphasizing expansion and contraction, emptying and filling, flowing and stillness, and the balance between them. I had the sense that Ken was watching me—his eyes were slightly open and he seemed to follow me as I moved. As I finished the dance, I experienced the relief that always comes to me through dancing, a letting go of the tensions I'm carrying, as I came more fully and peacefully into the present moment.

Kevin woke up and took his turn at the vigil. I changed into my nightgown and put on a red velvet robe that Ken had given me. It was an exact replica of one worn by Sally Field in a movie we'd seen together. I told myself I should try and get some sleep, but I couldn't allow myself to leave Ken for that long. His breathing had become quite noisy, making a watery sound as he breathed through an oxygen mask.

Kevin and I sat together on a sofa at the other end of the room from Ken's bed. Remembering some of my experience with Rose, I said out loud, "I wonder what his guide looks like? Rose told me that there was one in her room and that he had come to take her across to her new life. I thought, "I wonder if my brother Kenny might be Ken's guide, or my mother. Neither of them got to know Ken as a grown-up, but maybe that doesn't matter now."

Kevin said, "Being with Rose might not help you in being with Ken, Mom."

"It's harder," I admitted, "but it was helpful going through Rose's transition. I remember Rose's son describing the Buddhist belief that in the process of dying, the soul is constructing an energy body to move into when the person crosses.

Kevin was sitting with his back to Ken and without turning, he said, "I can just see what is going on in that side of the room. Ken's spirit is getting so big, it's too big for his body, and it's filling this room."

As he spoke, I too became aware of the energy in the room and the sense of something rising toward the high ceiling. I took a big breath and sighed, and my mouth opened involuntarily. I felt something coming into my body through my mouth, filling my chest and moving up my windpipe, opening my throat and causing me to gulp and shudder. I thought about the fact that Ken, as my son, had come *from* my body. Now it felt like part of the spirit that was Ken had entered me. A sense of comfort and peace came over me, which was puzzling.

Ken's breathing became quieter and more relaxed. "Maybe Ken is letting go more," I suggested.

"Or maybe he's just real comfortable where he is," Kevin said with a slight smile.

We crossed the room and came around Ken's bed to sit close. We looked at the clock as moonlight from a full moon began streaming through the front window high above us. It was after one thirty, in the early morning of the summer solstice. There was a knock on the front door. Kevin let Maureen in and then went for a drink of water in the kitchen.

Maureen came around the side of the bed, laying a nightshirt across Ken's bedding and in her characteristically flamboyant fashion said, "Here it is: the latest fashion in hospital gowns!" She took Ken's hand in hers and said, "I'm not getting much of a pulse."

As our eyes met, we realized it wasn't going to be long now. We changed positions and I called out for Kevin, but he didn't hear me. I thought about going to get Richard, who was asleep in the next room, but I couldn't bring myself to leave. Ken took a couple more breaths and that was it. I was holding his hand.

I placed my other hand on Ken's bare chest. His face was turned toward me. I removed the plastic mask from his mouth and nose and began intoning a prayer from my Catholic school upbringing. I was surprised how easily and powerfully it came to me. "Hail Mary, full of grace. . .Holy Mary, Mother of God, pray for us sinners, now and at the hour of our death."

Standing over the body of my son, an image came to me of Michelangelo's sculpture *Pietà*, the broken body of the crucified Jesus lying in the lap of his mother after being taken down from the cross. I felt a connection to Mary and to all the mothers whose sons' broken dead bodies have been delivered to their laps after war, famine, and disease.

>>> ■ <<<

Shortly after Ken died, I mentioned to Maureen the experience I'd had of Ken's energy entering my body. Her response was, "Oh, sure," like everyone knew about that, and she mentioned a name for it, which didn't stick with me. Later, when I asked her about it, she didn't remember the exchange and didn't know what I was talking about. Recently, I went to Google and typed in "moments near death." I found a reference from the *Encyclopedia of Death and Dying* to the "death flash," a sense that an energy has been passed from the dying person to a companion. The account stated, "This phenomenon has not been successfully studied but has experiential validity for those who feel they have been part of a mysterious transfer." I only know that it was such a vivid body experience that I can still relive it by just putting myself back in that moment.

CELEBRATIONS
OF KEN

"I choose you," I said to my eighty-five-year-old father as my four siblings and two adult children were thrashing around my house trying to get ready for Ken's memorial service. The house was bursting with creative commotion. We'd all been going through boxes of family photographs, selecting favorites and then arranging them on poster boards. Intended as a photo gallery of Ken's life, the photos would be displayed in the back of the ritual space at his memorial. It was time to leave to pick up Ken's ashes from the funeral home. "I choose you to come with me, Dad. You're the quietest one, and you're ready."

Dad had driven from Florida to Texas, a last-minute change in his itinerary. My sister Pat was in Florida to help Dad close the condo and return both cars to Detroit, where Dad spent the summers. I'd called him in Florida the previous Saturday morning.

"I wasn't sure I'd catch you. I thought you might already be on the road by now."

"Yeah, I don't know why we're not," he said with a tone of exasperation in his voice. "Patricia is moving pretty slow this morning. Not sure what's taking so long to get this show on the road." Then he interrupted himself, "But you're probably not calling with good news."

"No, Dad. Ken died early this morning at one forty-five on the summer solstice."

"Ohh, honey," he responded, with a quaver in his voice that reminded me I was *his* little girl. "Just a minute," he said and stepped away from the phone. As I waited at my end, I wondered where he'd gone, hoping he was okay. After what seemed longer than it probably was, he finally came back and I heard him rustling papers. "According to my map, if we leave in the next few minutes, we can drive to Jacksonville, turn left, and come across to Texas. We should be in Dallas by late Sunday afternoon."

And they got here right on schedule. In the next couple of days, other relatives arrived from Nebraska, Seattle, Nevada, Kentucky, Michigan, and Dallas. Through the kindness of Ken's boss, the service was being held at the American Airlines Conference Center. Rich's and George's relatives would fly from Illinois and Arizona into the airport nearby in time for the service and then take the next flight home.

Dad and I got into his car, and he began backing out of the driveway. His foot slipped off the brake and onto the accelerator, and the car lurched and swerved, taking out several of our neighbor's shrubs alongside the driveway. We were stuck. The neighbors and our relatives gathered around, and someone located a shovel and dug the car out of the mud. Dad seemed relatively calm, even in this circumstance, but I realized this accident showed that he too was experiencing a lot of stress.

Eventually, my family got organized enough to make it to the conference center pretty much on time, which is not a family specialty, even in stress-free times. Dad's assault on the neighbor's landscape delayed us, but thankfully he and I were able to get to the mortuary, pick up Ken's ashes, and arrive at the center before any of the guests. I wrapped a thick golden cord around the black plastic box that contained Ken's ashes. It made the box resemble a gift, and I placed it on the table in the front of the room. The cord was a symbol in honor of Ken's crying out, in the last hours of his life, "I need more rope."

On the table next to the ashes, I placed a portrait of Ken with the family dog, Sasha, a large white furry Samoyed, the third dog of its breed who'd been a beloved member of our family. Seeing the dog reminded me of our first Samoyed, Samantha, who grew up with the kids and became quite elderly and infirm about the time the two older ones went off to college. At the end of each visit home from school, Corinne and Kevin would turn to the dog. Pointing a commanding finger at her, they would say, "Good-bye, Samantha. Don't die till I get back."

Samantha's end came when Ken was a senior in high school. Rich and I were out of town when Ken realized Samantha was in distress. She was bleeding from somewhere, so he wrapped her in a towel, put her in the backseat of his car, and drove to the vet. She died on the way. We had her cremated, and the next time the whole family was together we held a ceremony. Ken had dug a hole in the corner of the backyard, and the five of us stood around telling our special memories of her. As I recall, my irreverent son Ken got the last word. After shoveling the dirt over her grave, he said, in his most commanding voice, "Stay, Samantha. Stay."

>>> ■ <<<

While living with AIDS, Ken attended a number of friends' memorials. He talked about what he'd liked about those services and always mentioned the flowers. A friend of Ken and Les's was a florist who provided arrangements for many of Dallas's high-end hotels. He volunteered to get the flowers wholesale and donate his labor, but he needed my help with the cost of the materials. I agreed, having no idea what I was signing up for. When I saw what he and his friends had created, I was overwhelmed with the beauty of their artwork. Two elegant, bountiful bouquets of fresh flowers stood six feet tall on either side of the raised platform where the ceremony would be held. Another matching bouquet sat on a round table in the vestibule—greeting everyone as they entered and signed the roster. The flowers transformed the atmosphere of the utilitarian conference space into a place of enchantment.

A video screen would be used to play an excerpt of one of Ken's musical theater performances. This possibility came about at the last minute when I heard from his college theater professor. She'd made copies of several of Ken's solos in the musicals she'd directed and gave them to me as a gift. I learned later that she had already done this several times for other students' mothers whose sons had died of AIDS. I wondered how well Ken knew them.

Looking out over the crowd, I smiled at the diversity and multicultural nature of the gathering. Besides close family members and friends of Ken's, some of whom had put together the order of the program, there were fellow employees of the hotel, many of them Mexican American; members of the extended Dallas gay community; professional colleagues from our clinic, some of whom did not know Ken personally; women from my spirituality group; and our neighbors and friends.

As the service was about to begin, I stood in the back of the room with Glenda, who would be presiding as the minister. I felt tears of stage fright, exhaustion, and sorrow starting to break through my composure. Then I heard Ken's upbeat theater voice inside me say, "You can cry tomorrow, Mom. It's show time!" This made me laugh and ready to perform.

The service began with one of Ken's favorite songs, sung by the Heartsong Gay Men's Chorus, whose members were all HIV positive. "One voice, singing in the darkness, all it takes is one voice. One voice, and soon there's more than one voice."

Glenda offered the opening prayer. I later transcribed it from the video of the service because her words offered me much hope. To be reminded in this time of such immense loss that I could still be connected to Ken through the love I had for him was something I longed to believe.

Let us pray.

Divine Spirit, everywhere present, in whom we live and have our being. We come together tonight to honor Kenneth

Collins. We give thanks for the great gift of knowing him. We seek comfort in our sorrow at the loss of his physical presence among us, and we acknowledge the everlasting life of his spirit. Grant that we may live in such a way that we continue to be present to him and to the love we have for him, all our days, until we too, like Kenneth, leave behind the limitations of our body and move freely on, into larger life. Amen.

Ken's service had much in common with a theatrical performance, partly because it was a celebration of Ken's life and his love of theater was central to his vitality. And many of Ken's friends and family members were theater performers. Corinne had sung at many weddings, including her own. "I'd love to sing for Ken," she said at the planning meeting, "but being seven months pregnant doesn't improve a singer's breath control. Plus, I'm afraid I might just start crying mid-song and not be able to finish."

Her cousin Heather, also a singer, had put her arm around Corinne and offered to help. So the two of them stood side by side, Corinne singing the lead in her light soprano voice and Heather singing harmony and supporting the song through the tough places of "Amazing Grace."

It's hard now to imagine where I got the courage, but I danced at Ken's service. I had danced at Rose's service at her request, even though at the time I'd never really heard of anyone dancing at a funeral. But judging from that experience, it seemed fitting that I should dance at Kenneth's. I used an improvisational InterPlay form that alternates dancing and storytelling. As I began to move, my body felt heavy, my feet cemented to the ground, but as I moved the dance created a lightness in my being. A minute or so into the dance, I heard the voice of my three-and-a-half-year-old grandson, William, who was seated with his parents in the front row. He called out in a loud stage whisper, "What is she doing?"

I stopped and went over to him. "I'm dancing for Uncle Ken. Do you want to dance too?" He shook his head and buried his face in his mother's sleeve. But five-and-a-half-year-old Ethan got up without hesitation and joined me. We danced together, at first holding hands, and then he was in my arms as I lifted him up and we both twirled round and round. I felt pure joy, the joy that children bring us, the joy that Ken had brought me.

After I put Ethan down and he returned to his seat by his parents, I continued moving, and I saw in my mind's eye an image of the conventional way people's birth and death dates are written, always with a dash in between. Ken was born on April Fools' Day and he died on the summer solstice. So my dance and story moved across the space, from side to side. "From April Fools' to the summer solstice . . . from April Fools' to the summer solstice." It came to me that it's the dash that counts. No matter how long or short a life, it's the *quality* of the dash that counts. The dash was shorter than I would have wanted it to be, but a feeling of gratitude welled up in me, for the richness of Ken's life and for the richness he brought into mine.

Corinne went next, telling her story of how Ken always went the extra mile. "When I was a college student," Corinne began, "probably in depression about not hearing from my boyfriend (now my husband), Ken wanted to cheer me up. He was a high school student who didn't drive a car yet, but he had an unlicensed moped motorcycle. After we talked on the phone, he baked some chocolate chip cookies and got them to me by driving the fifteen miles from Arlington to the TCU campus in Fort Worth entirely on the service roads." She concluded her comments with, "Ken's in heaven with all the other people that we love, and he's taking care of my babies."

Ken's closest girlfriend, Patty, sang a song from *Sweeney Todd*, a show they'd performed together in college. His most intimate male friend, Les, told of how they met and then about the night Ken died. "I'd asked Sheila to call and let me know when he crossed. And she did call, but she called my work number, so I didn't get the message. She felt so bad, but it didn't matter, because it worked out perfectly. I've never had anything like this happen to me, but Ken came to me in a dream that night. He looked great and he said, 'Come with me.' I told him I couldn't, but I believe this was his way of letting me know he's fine." While Les was telling this story, I got chills thinking about the fact that the morning after Ken crossed, Les had had an auto accident that totaled his car, but he walked away unscathed. Now I know that when someone we love crosses, we must be careful not to follow him or her into death.

Kevin was the last to speak, and he brought a more sober mood to the proceedings. Holding a clipboard in his hand, he looked every bit his role of location manager in the film industry.

"My brother Ken was gay," he said in a strong voice. "My brother Ken died of AIDS." There were people in the audience who did not know one or both of these truths, especially people from Ken's work. "But I want to ask you, how should my brother be judged?

"Was he joyful? Was he kind? Was he considerate? Hardworking? He was all of those things. And I mourn for those who never knew him. And for those who are afraid to know a man like Ken. I was the last person my brother took care of. I was with him when he was dying, and he saw me crying. He reached over and comforted me. 'It's okay. Don't be sad.'"

Through the magic of technology, Ken performed at his own service. A youthful twenty-year-old Ken sang one of his favorite songs from *Oliver*, "Consider yourself at home, consider yourself one of the fam-i-ly. Consider yourself one of us." And it became so. Everyone in that room that evening became one of us.

When the service ended, I turned to Richard. "I wish we didn't ever have to leave here. There's so much love in this room. Every molecule of air is filled with it. I wish I could stay here the rest of my life."

Rich's remark has comforted me all the years since: "Well, that's where Ken is now."

>>> ■ <<<

The following summer, our family vacation included a trip to Detroit to inter Ken's ashes. Since we had relocated several times to different parts of the country when Ken was growing up, it was difficult to decide where to bury his ashes, but George's history-buff sister, Mary, helped us decide. She suggested a cemetery less than a mile from where we used to live that was closed to all but direct descendants of the early Detroiters buried there. Ken qualified, since his great-grandfather, Detroit's first school superintendent, was buried there alongside his great-grandmother, a school principal, and both of George's parents.

My side of the family had strong Detroit ties as well. My parents met and were married in Detroit, though we never lived there as kids. Eight months after George and I were married, we relocated to Detroit for George's dream job as a radio news broadcaster. All three kids were born there, and I'd gotten two of my degrees there. When I told our plans to Margaret, the woman who had been Ken's nanny, she was delighted that "he's coming home, where I can watch out for him."

The following week, which was the week of my birthday, we drove to northern Michigan, returning to a quaint time-share resort where we'd gone skiing.

It all seems of one piece in my memory: the almost-too-warm sunlight on my face as I stood talking with friends and family outside the Detroit mausoleum, the shimmer of the trees at the river's edge in my sister's backyard as I visited with cousins on her screened-in porch, the smell of the loamy earth in the woods of northern Michigan—a backdrop to watching my eleven-month-old granddaughter, Vitoria, standing proudly, carefully clutching the edge of a coffee table to move gingerly around the condo's living room.

Then there are the dramatic moments, the ones that stay in your heart forever: the feel of six-year-old Ethan's hand in mine as we danced together again in honor of Uncle Ken, our bare feet on the mausoleum's cool marble floor, the soft, enveloping feeling of Margaret's brown, sheltering arms as she hugged me with all her strength. And that never-to-be forgotten moment on my birthday, when Tori let go of the coffee table and took her first-ever steps alone, toward me, landing in my outstretched arms—the best birthday present ever.

>>> ▪ <<<

The memorial services and the connection with family and close friends were more than a temporary balm to my sorrow. These experiences seemed to soak into the ligaments of my ongoing life. From here on out, alongside the memories of Ken struggling with the discomforts and infirmities of his battle with AIDS, would be the memories of the love and support that came forward from our family and communities. Through the years, these memories have remained inseparable.

PART TWO

REACTING TO THE NEWS

On a Saturday morning in March, nearly five years after Ken's death, I was running late, driving to a Pilates class while admonishing myself, "There must be an exercise class closer than fifteen miles into Fort Worth." Driving past the clusters of oak trees in our subdivision, fed by the creek behind our house, I knew why we'd chosen to live there. It was these very trees that had drawn us off the interstate on our first visit to Texas. But still, being this far from town had its inconveniences. Just before I got to the main highway, my cell phone rang.

It was Corinne, calling from her home in Nebraska. With tenderness in her voice, she said, "I need to tell you, Mom, I've been diagnosed with breast cancer."

I felt my stomach drop below the floorboard of the car. I pulled over and stopped at the side of the road. Corinne gave me little chance to respond. "I found out late yesterday afternoon," she said, "but I waited until this morning to call you. Bill and I didn't get much sleep last night. I thought, No sense all of us being up all night."

She knew she needed to call this morning. She knew this diagnosis would impact all of us: immediately, her close and extended family; later on, her network of friends. And though she couldn't have imagined it then, eventually it would intrude into the lives of strangers she would never meet.

As I continued listening to the details of her situation, I appreciated what my daughter had been through in the last five years. Besides losing her brother to AIDS at age thirty-five, while pregnant with twins, she had found a tiny lump in her breast. The twins had not lived past the first term, and after they died in utero, a biopsy of the breast lump came back negative. Every six months since, as advised, she'd had a mammogram. Although Corinne continued to feel that something was wrong, nothing showed up on any of the tests, until now. And this biopsy was at her insistence, when she became determined enough to override the surgeon who told her, "You know you don't have cancer, so why worry about it?" I remembered her saying to me in January, "I hate that they look at me like a nutcase, but this breast is more swollen than the other one. Okay, so it isn't cancer, but it is *something*. And I am going to insist they find out what it is."

I continued listening on my cell phone to the details Corinne was providing. The cancer was "stage three because of the size"; "not likely to have spread." There would be surgery followed by radiation. I pictured my beautiful, blonde daughter, a physical therapist who'd been training for a triathlon in celebration of her fortieth birthday. I thought of the injustice of it, and I thought of Wilma, Corinne's mother-in-law.

For most of Corinne and Bill's married life—through finding, moving into, and fixing up houses; through vacations and new jobs; through the birth of each of their children—in the background and foreground was the trauma and treatment of Wilma's breast cancer. As her family support system, they accompanied her nine-year journey through chemotherapy and radiation; her recurring decisions about balancing the benefits and risks of each proposed new treatment; her enduring suffering, discomfort, and illness in the hope of gaining more healthy time. And somehow for all those years, she beat the odds. Finally, a year and a half after the loss of Corinne's twins, six months after Corinne's youngest child, Vitoria, was born, Wilma died.

Still holding my phone to my ear, I drove slowly the few blocks back home to find Rich working on bills at a small desk in our living room. Not expecting me home so soon, and seeing the expression on my face, he knew something was very wrong. "Just a minute, Corinne." I interrupted our conversation. "Corinne has been diagnosed with breast cancer," I told him, and the horror on his face mirrored what was happening in my insides.

By this point, Corinne's phone conversation had turned to wanting a double mastectomy. "After what Wilma went through, I just want an end to the threat of this disease hanging over our heads." Rich grabbed the phone from me and began talking with Corinne, while I thought, "How odd. In my day, the furor was over too many unnecessary mastectomies."

>>> ■ <<<

I brought Rich into Corinne's life when she was thirteen, but they bonded strongly her senior year in high school when, several months after we married, I accepted a teaching job in Texas. Rich had to stay in Nebraska to finish his dissertation, so while her brothers came with me, Corinne chose to stay with Rich to finish high school. She understood the family move was strongly influenced by the free college tuition for my children that would be a perk of my new university job and that she would be the first beneficiary. Still, she often teased, "She married him, and I got to live with him."

In the swirl of activity that followed that phone call, Rich called his physician brother, a radiologist, and they repeated medical terms and discussed opinions. Surgery versus chemotherapy? With the size of the tumor, she would need both. But in what order? A new study on the Internet suggested that chemotherapy first might be better. The chemo shrinks the tumor so there isn't as much left for the surgeon to do. From what we learned, we supported Corinne and Bill in getting a second opinion at a major medical center.

Two weeks later, Rich and I flew from Texas to Kansas City and drove to Lincoln, arriving in time for lunch with four-year-old Tori.

Rich and I took her to a restaurant named Grandmother's, and we laughed together at the name and how this had to be the exact right place for us to eat. We sat in a small booth with high sides and a single lamp suspended over the table, providing privacy and a sense of intimacy. After ordering lunch, we asked Tori what was new in *her* life.

Leaning over and in a stage whisper, being sure to correctly pronounce her words, she said, "Mommy has been diagnosed with breast cancer." "But we can help her," she quickly added. "Aunt Debbie says that she can use lots of hugs and that will make her feel much better." Later, when we told Corinne and Bill what Tori had said, Rich and I agreed with Bill's response, "Wouldn't it be great to take things in stride like she does."

A day or so later, we drove with Corinne and Bill the sixty miles to the medical center in Omaha, where I had been with Rose, for a second opinion consultation. An all-business, fifty-something woman physician met with us after she had examined Corinne and reviewed the records and scans we had rounded up from labs all over Lincoln to bring with us. Thanks to the Internet, we knew more about her than she knew about us. We knew she served on a national panel that decides on recommended treatments and protocols for the many diseases that make up what we call breast cancer.

"I've just gotten back from a conference in Florida," she began. Our confidence in her grew as she spoke, because that's where the study we'd read about was presented. "A new study was reported that reversed what we have been recommending. The women who had chemotherapy first, followed by surgery, did better. In some instances, the chemo shrank the tumor so extensively there was little left for surgery." Based on that new information, that was her recommendation. "That'd be great. Less for surgery to do," I thought.

We left the medical center satisfied that we'd received the most up-to-date information from a professional who knew what she was talking about. The doctor's vita on the Internet, her position on the

National Advisory Committee on Breast Cancer, her professional tone, even her dispassionate manner all served to reassure us. We were on the right path. We were doing the right thing.

But as I fastened my seat belt and settled into the backseat of the car for the ride home, I realized something the doctor had said was still with me. I'd asked a simple question about a treatment alternative. "And what if that doesn't work?" The doctor had answered, unemotionally, "Then you die of your disease."

This phrase kept ringing in my ears as the car slowly maneuvered down the spiral exit ramp of the parking structure. In spite of our experience with Wilma and my best friend Rose, both of whom had "died of their disease," I had not allowed myself to consider this possibility for Corinne.

After hearing of Corinne's diagnosis, showers became my venting chambers. No matter where I was staying, the tiny stalls, usually enclosed by glass doors and surrounding tile, provided soundproofing for my howling rage. "WHAT GOOD CAN COME FROM THIS?" I sang to the universe. As an InterPlay teacher, I often helped people get comfortable with their singing voices, and singing in the shower is one way that I became comfortable with mine. Like the flexible showerhead that can double the force of the water spray, or intermittently pulse it, I waited for the song phrase to move around, as it often did, and bring me to a softer place. But "WHAT GOOD CAN COME FROM THIS?" wasn't budging.

>>> ■ <<<

Rich and I were scheduled to go to Australia with twenty other American InterPlayers. Unlike my first husband, whose theme song had been "I won't dance; don't ask me," Richard frequently joined me in my involvements with dance and the performance arts. Shortly after we met, we traveled together to study community rituals with Anna Halprin. Later, while co-directing our behavioral health care clinic, we took ballroom dancing lessons as our weekly TGIF activity, and we became involved in InterPlay, an expressive arts system based in movement.

Corinne insisted we go; staying home and forfeiting our plane tickets would gain nothing. With that encouragement, we stuck with our plans, and after a thirteen-hour flight, we met up with thirty Australian InterPlayers. We played together for a week using the improvisational InterPlay forms of singing, dancing, and storytelling in preparation for two theater performances at a university on the theme of the *Unbelievable Beauty of Being Human.*

The original four performances of *Unbelievable Beauty* were held in San Francisco in 1997, the fall after Ken died. I still remember both the terror and excitement I felt, holding that invitational postcard in my hand. I knew what Ken would have said had he been alive. He would insist that I do it. That conviction gave me the courage to participate in his honor. So here I was, in the midst of another traumatic circumstance, this time involving my daughter. And here were two InterPlay *Unbelievable Beauty of Being Human* performances, where our own stories are the stuff with which we create.

Even using the same format, each InterPlay performance is unique. The director gathers the words generated by the audience on the overall theme and then weds them to the InterPlay forms, a particular type of song, dance, or storytelling. If a member of the cast has an idea for something he or she wants to do, the director usually includes that in the show. During the first week of our time in Australia, we rehearsed the forms, toured the sights of Sydney, and swapped stories around the kitchen table with our home-stay hosts, who were mural artists. All the while, my stomach reminded me that all was not well in my world. I sampled the pumpkin soup in every Australian restaurant we visited, as recommended by our Aussie friends. It's their version of our chicken soup. I finally had to admit that my stomach wasn't going to let me forget the recent events that had unsettled my family's life and my own. Before the second performance, my discomfort grew bigger than my fear of doing something about it, and I told the director, "*I need* to sing a song for Corinne."

Cynthia knew that singing in public was outside my comfort zone. Going to that place in the presence of an audience during a performance is not usually recommended, but she trusted my intuition as to what I needed—my body's wisdom, as we call it in InterPlay.

During the show, we had explored some juicy good stuff about being human that people in the audience had called out for us: naps, grandchildren, chocolate, back rubs. And mixed in were pieces inspired by the not-so-good stuff: taxes, job layoffs, bills. And then we got to cancer. That was my cue. Cynthia stationed me downstage, next to the musicians, and called for volunteers from the company to dance to the song I was about to create.

Just like in the shower, I began with my eyes closed, in a somewhat timid but deep and angry voice: "What *GOOD*, what *GOOD*, what *GOOD* can come from *THIS*?" My voice got stronger when I heard the instrumentalists following my rhythm. "What *GOOD*, what *GOOD*, what *GOOD* can come from *THIS*?" I caught sight of the dancers and realized that one of them was Richard, who was as worried about Corinne as I was.

"What *GOOD*, what *GOOD*, what *GOOD* can come from *THIS*?"

And then the song began to change. In the Greek tradition of stage as altar, and dance and theater as healing arts, a softening came into my voice, into my whole body. The song became a prayer: "*GOOD can* come from this, *GOOD can* come from this." The prayer turned into pledge and promise, "*GOOD WILL* COME FROM THIS. GOOD. WILL. COME. FROM. THIS!" In the aftermath, as the song resonated throughout my body, I began to feel, for the first time, that it would.

>>> ■ <<<

As I did with Ken, once I got over my rage, I resolved to walk with Corinne on whatever path her life was asking her to take. And in preparing for her treatment, the first stop needed to be a wig shop. She and eight-year-old William had had a special conversation about the changes that might happen due to her diagnosis, and he told her, "I don't like to see ladies with bald heads." Will's concern came from his experience with his other grandmother, who, during the later years of her cancer treatment, didn't always wear her wig around the house. Corinne promised Will he wouldn't have to see her bald head, so we headed to a wig expert at a beauty parlor outfitted in the art deco style of my mother's era. I thought about all the women who had consulted with her in the past thirty years and was glad we were in the hands of a professional who knew her business.

The visit was especially bittersweet when she shared memories of Wilma. "It was the love of her grandchildren and wanting to be there for more of their lives that kept her going," she said. I thought of how I'd envied Wilma, living in the same town with our grandchildren, and I guess she envied me, being the "away grandmother" who was seen as special company when I visited. But I never wanted to change places with her, given her set of unrelenting health challenges.

Corinne recounted an incident when Wilma had become discouraged and told her she was considering not taking any more treatments. "I'd just come from the doctors, where I'd learned I was pregnant. I hadn't even told my husband yet. I listened to her politely, but I thought to myself, 'When you find out about another grandchild on the way, you'll be signing up for those treatments.' And of course she did."

Corinne had heard about an organization, Locks of Love, to which people donate their hair for use in making wigs for children undergoing chemotherapy. "I definitely want to do that if my hair is long enough."

Taking out her ruler, the wig lady measured Corinne's hair. "You will have a short bob in the back, but you definitely have enough hair to donate. And the quality and color of your hair will match many young children's natural hair."

For the second appointment to pick up the wig and donate the hair, we brought Tori. She was so excited to be included in this special grown-up excursion that she allowed me to brush her hair and add barrettes without protesting as I got her ready. Tori sat on a chair next to her mother, legs dangling, hardly taking her eyes off Corinne as she tried on the new wig that was to become hers. She joked and played dress-up to Tori's delight as the wig lady demonstrated stylish looks that could be achieved with headbands, scarves, and the new wig. After the wig had been styled to fit Corinne's face, and tips for its care spelled out, it was time to cut twelve inches off her beautiful blonde hair.

A few snips of the scissors and the haircut was done. A few more minutes trimming the straggly stray ends in the back, and Corinne's dramatic new look was complete. "If only the rest of her journey with breast cancer could be that easy," I thought, as I saw a glimpse of my elementary-school-age daughter who'd had that short bob hairdo. As we left to go pick up the brothers at their elementary school, Tori skipped to the van in excitement, clearly delighted that she got to be there when the deed was done.

After we pulled into the driveway of the school, my grandsons piled into the backseat of the van, backpacks and school papers flying. I was sitting in the front next to Corinne, who was driving. Tori sat in her car seat in the third row. After fastening his seat belt, William looked up at the back of his mother's head and shouted out in horror, "Your hair is *too short*. It's UGLY!"

"Now, William," I said in what sounded like, even to me, an inane grandmother voice, "that isn't a very nice thing to say to your mother."

But Tori had no trouble responding decisively and with authority. In her most grown-up, bossy voice, she said, "IT'S FOR THE CHILDREN. She had to cut it short so she could give her hair to the CHILDREN!"

Then, in the silence that followed, she asked slowly and thoughtfully from her seat in the back of the van, "How do children get cancer? They don't have breasts!"

DREAMS AND
THE KINDNESS
OF STRANGERS

Cell phones, video conferencing, satellite radio, and the World Wide Web: I try to keep up. The world seems both a smaller and much larger place than what I knew growing up. I'd been getting plenty of advice from lots of people since Corinne's treatment for breast cancer wasn't working. We'd moved from the common starting point of, "Oh, God, isn't it awful to have breast cancer" to "Oh, God, the tumor is resisting the chemotherapy? How could this be?" Friends and family, and their friends and family members, all seemed to know some treatment that had worked for someone in spite of the odds or the regulations of the Food and Drug Administration.

In 2002, the year of Corinne's diagnosis, people conducted searches on computers in their own homes, finding information about medical conditions, diagnoses, drugs, clinical trials, and alternative treatments and methods of healing, most with testimonies from satisfied patients who had benefited from the various protocols. Early on Corinne had asked me, "Get on the computer *for* me and find out what there is out there. It's just too overwhelming to read all that stuff and keep track of it."

What she didn't say was something I had trouble with as well. It's extremely discouraging to read research reports celebrating a gain of four or five months of life for the treatment group versus the placebo group when that small gain doesn't come anywhere near the thirty or forty years of life we're hoping for.

And hope was extremely important to Corinne, who as a physical therapist was first and foremost a cheerleader for her patients' recovery. She was adamant in not allowing anyone, particularly a doctor, to take her hope away. "My ob-gyn said he's had many patients diagnosed with breast cancer through the years, and they're all doing fine now. He told me, 'I'm sure you'll be rocking your grandchildren.' That gave me hope when he said that. And if he turns out to be wrong, what's the problem? I'm not gonna get mad and sue him."

When Corinne's first chemotherapy treatment failed, I had a dream, the setting of which was a large casino. Since the time in my late teens when I had worked in Las Vegas as a dancer, I have always *hated* casinos. In the dream I recognized the black velvety walls, the beep and flash of the pulsing electronic signage, the *clang* and *ka-ching* of the slot machines. Struggling to see through the smoke-filled air and techno-freaky lighting, I am finally able to make out the figures of Corinne and other members of our family playing at a blackjack table. Over the stacks of chips on the green table, I see a sign that reads, High-Tech Science. As the stack of chips dwindles, it's clear we are losing badly. Looking around, I notice people playing other games at other tables configured differently. I feel an impulse to suggest that we try our hand at one of the other tables. But since I don't know the rules or the odds, I'm afraid to mention it.

Waking from the dream, I realized that all anyone really wants to know about any treatment, whatever the odds given, is "Where do *I* fall among your categories? What are *my* odds? Who wouldn't sign up immediately, whether the statistics reported on a treatment's effectiveness are 30 percent, 10 percent, or even 1 percent, if they could be assured they'd be in the group for which the treatment *works*? And that's the one thing no one can ever tell you.

Reflecting on my dream, I thought of the trip we had taken to get a second opinion in Omaha before Corinne began treatment.

Playing the "what if" game patients and family members play with themselves when things go wrong in the treatment journey, I wondered, what if we *hadn't* consulted with the Medical Center in Omaha? Might things have turned out better? Corinne would have had surgery first (perhaps a double mastectomy at her own insistence), followed by the traditional chemotherapy treatment Epirubicin Cytoxan, also known as the red devil for the way it colors the patient's urine and produces severe side effects. Corinne had this treatment along with Cytoxan, and the drug, Taxatere, for a total of twelve weeks, and she did suffer nausea and vomiting each of the four times it was administered. From what we know now, these drugs wouldn't have done much for her, but she wouldn't have known that, because the only way to track its effects, via the tumor and/or her breasts, would have been removed by the surgery. For some period, Corinne would be merrily back to her normal life, or the "new normal" that cancer patients hope to achieve after surviving treatment and the threat to their lives.

But of course, with three of the four of us in the health care field ourselves, a physical therapist, a psychologist, a social worker, and a banker with an MBA, there was no way we *wouldn't* have gotten a second opinion, and followed along with whatever was suggested. So Corinne had the chemotherapies first, before any surgery. But when her cancer proved resistant to the chemicals she couldn't get to surgery. Ninety percent of patients respond to these drugs, but Corinne's cancer didn't.

And for the oddsmakers, there was Corinne's supposed chance of ever getting breast cancer in the first place: One doctor told her before her diagnosis, "Ninety to ninety-nine percent chance it isn't cancer." Another doctor said, when discouraging a biopsy she had asked for to address her concern for the swelling in her breast, "You know you don't have cancer, you have *no risk factors.*" I wondered why Corinne would be willing to continue playing at this table at all. Much later I saw a sign on the trail of a Race for the Cure: "*Every* woman is at risk for breast cancer." Since that time, I've made it my mission to pass that truth on to every woman I meet.

>>> ■ <<<

Given that Corinne's cancer was not behaving as most do, Rich and I felt it was time to get Corinne to a world-class cancer center. We knew people who had gone to M.D. Anderson in Houston with good results, and we could get her in quickly if one of her Nebraska doctors was willing to ask for a *third* opinion. Rich and I understood from Corinne that her doctor was not in favor of the idea of a trip to Houston, perhaps feeling it would be an expensive "wild goose chase." But Rich and I persisted, doubling our efforts after Rich's phone conversation with one of her doctors. He agreed to sign the papers but he said, "You can go to Houston, but it won't make any difference in the outcome. I knew when I diagnosed her, her fate was sealed."

This statement made Rich extremely angry, and though he shared it with me, we elected to not tell Corinne and Bill. We weren't ready to give up hope and we didn't want to take away their hope that something could be done for her. We drove the four hours from Fort Worth and met Corinne and Bill at the Houston Airport, a trip I would make many more times in the following year. We stayed initially in a hotel owned by the center, located just across the street from its hospital and clinics. It was a high-end establishment, providing convenience and sensitive service to the many patients and their families who travel long distances for diagnostic and cancer treatments. Crossing the street to the clinic building, we were impressed by the prominent placement of the Integrative Medicine Clinic, just to the right of the front entrance. In truth, when we first heard of this clinic, we expected it to be located in a trailer out back in the parking lot. We took encouragement from the signs and flyers promoting the yoga, Pilates, and nutrition classes, since both Corinne and I saw exercise and nutrition as important parts of our own health care. We would take advantage of many of these classes later on, but on our first visit, we were kept busy navigating the many clinics and specialists that make up the treatment teams of this world-renowned institution.

After much poking, prodding, and scanning, we awaited the verdict in a spacious, well-appointed reception area beside a six-foot-high fish tank. Bill worked on the community crossword puzzle spread out on a large table, as many husbands before him had most likely done. Rich thumbed through recent magazines and restlessly explored the adjoining hallways.

I sat next to Corinne, trying to stay in my social worker mindset, supporting my daughter while she blew her nose into a handful of tissues. "There are probably 400 cancer patients in this building, and I am the only one crying."

An aproned, thirty-something volunteer overhead Corinne's comment and introduced herself as a cancer survivor. "I've cried. We all have, and we will again," she said, offering Corinne a reassuring hug and another tissue. And as happened frequently with Corinne, there began a beautiful friendship.

"You are not a candidate for surgery at this time," the physicians all agreed. Getting to surgery would only be possible once a successful course of chemotherapy had been accomplished. She was invited to participate in a clinical trial of a secret-formula drug given just prior to each chemotherapy treatment. The new drug was designed to help the chemotherapy stay in the cells longer. Chemotherapy drugs are undeniably poison, so the theory was that perhaps some people have particularly strong pumps on their cells that eliminate the chemotherapy too quickly, interfering with its ability to work on the cancer. As in all scientific experiments, all other variables needed to remain the same, so Corinne traveled to Houston one day a week to receive the same chemotherapy drug that had not worked previously in Nebraska. But this time, each dosage was preceded by the secret-formula one.

Surveying the northern and western Houston skylines from our elegant corner hotel suite, I thought to myself, "Ken would definitely approve." As a concierge at four-star hotels in the Dallas area, Ken had always believed that everyone deserved the best when they traveled: the best décor, the best convenience, and something he always saw to—the best service. And Corinne and I had all that at this beautiful historic hotel, recently restored to its 1920s grandeur. The most amazing part: the room was provided complimentary to us on each visit. We were traveling to Houston often in those days that Corinne participated in the clinical trial. The trials were available to patients whose hometown treatments had failed to work and who remained healthy enough to undergo them. The routine was: Corinne would fly from Nebraska once a week, going and returning in a single day, often on airline miles donated by friends. While she was traveling, she would write e-mail updates to friends and family to avoid the catch-up phone calls, which took her away from time with her children when she returned home. Every month or so, when it was time for testing to see how the treatment was working, I would drive the four hours from my home in Fort Worth to join her.

The benefactor for our hotel room lived in New York City and had never met Corinne. His company had just purchased a hotel near the Texas Medical Center in Houston when he began reading the e-mail journal Corinne wrote as she traveled back and forth. It was forwarded to him by his mother, one of Rich's friends. He told his mother, "This kid could use a break," and he offered Corinne the gift of a free hotel room whenever she needed it, along with one for visiting family members at a reduced rate. I was amazed at how Corinne was attracting supporters and what kindness and generosity these strangers, or friends of friends, offered her.

One Saturday morning, Corinne and I were relaxing in our elegant Houston hotel suite, recovering from three days of stressful tests and consultations at the hospital clinics. We'd decided to stay over till Monday because Corinne couldn't do chemo the prior week; her counts were too low. We began watching the breaking news on CNN, hoping to see the first pictures of the space shuttle *Columbia* and its multiple vapor trails over Texas. Houston has strong connections to the aerospace industry, so I imagine many locals were doing just what we were doing that morning. Rich had called from Fort Worth to remind us to turn on the TV. He was talking on his cell phone while standing in a clearing a few blocks from our house, hoping for an unobstructed view of the shuttle's reentry path over Fort Worth.

But as we watched, things began to go terribly wrong. We heard the announcer's voice explaining what we were viewing as "disintegration over Texas during reentry." Seconds later: "Shuttle scattering its remains from Fort Worth to East Texas, Arkansas, and Louisiana." We gasped in disbelief as the horror being transmitted over the screen reverberated throughout our bodies. Seven people's lives disintegrated; seven families and a nation shattered. The details of our personal soap opera disappeared into the background as we hugged one another and said silent prayers for all those involved.

>>> ■ <<<

"You Really Can Prevent Cancer" the signs at M.D. Anderson Cancer Center proclaimed. In the interest of patient education, I assume, these signs were placed on the back of the door of every women's restroom on the campus of the world-class medical center. In colorful bold graphics, the sign exhibited two columns of lists. The first, under the heading "Healthy Lifestyle Behaviors," included reminders to eat fruits and vegetables, avoid smoking, exercise regularly, limit time in the sun, and a bonus suggestion: "Know your family's history of cancer." The second, the "Early Detection Can Help" list, named various types of cancer and the age at which you should have particular screenings by health care professionals.

The problem with this sign? It was a bold-faced lie. And we women going in and out of these necessary facilities several times a day knew that better than anyone. Most of us were already cancer patients or friends and family members of cancer patients. Most women patients we met at the center, like my daughter, had lived healthy lifestyles and had had medical screening even earlier than the experts' standard recommendations. And not having a family history of breast cancer worked against Corinne. Her concerns were not taken seriously until a blind biopsy done at her insistence a few days after her fortieth birthday revealed stage 3 breast cancer.

And I was sure, if we asked the center's 600 researchers, 800 nurses, and 150 cafeteria workers, they would agree that *none* of the healthy behaviors listed have been *proven* to prevent cancer. These behaviors might *contribute* to a strong, healthy body, which would come in handy if and when you needed to be treated for cancer. As my daughter and I had been learning, as long as you're healthy, you can try yet another aggressive treatment regime to fight your cancer. And while early screening might increase your chances of *surviving* various types of cancer, screenings do not *prevent* cancer; they only provide confirmation of it. This sign went way beyond the available scientific data.

So the sign became a frequent topic of conversation among the patients and family members as we sat together for hours on end in the hospital waiting rooms. We discussed how, even in a situation where someone's cancer might have been prevented—say, in the case of a long-term smoker who'd developed lung cancer—this would hardly be the time to rub it in.

My personal reaction to the sign and its scientific errors escalated through the many months we visited the center—from mild annoyance, to resentment at being insulted, to anger. With repeated exposure, I became concerned that its message fed the guilt feelings, self-blame, and depression that often accompany a cancer diagnosis and treatment journey. Patients invariably ask themselves, "Why did this happen to *me*?" "Am I being punished for something I've done or failed to do?" "Should I have stuck to a vegetarian diet?" "Taken my vitamins more regularly?"

Since my daughter and I and our friends and family members traveled to M.D. Anderson frequently and regularly for a year and a half, frequently and regularly we saw this insulting sign. One day, after learning that the clinical trial treatment she was participating in was having no effect on her cancer, Corinne took her pinkish-red lipstick and wrote the word "NOT" over the plastic frame. We relished that small victory: in that one restroom at least, for a short time, the sign read, "You Really Can NOT Prevent Cancer."

With the failure of Corinne's trial treatment, we earned an invitation to the *Extremely* High-Tech Experimental Gambling Table. Corinne was asked to consider a bone marrow transplant, provided that a suitable donor could be located. Bone marrow transplants had been proven effective with some blood cancers like leukemia, but for breast cancer it was a highly experimental procedure. Corinne prayed for guidance as her biological family members—Kevin, George, and I—had tests to see if we were enough of a match to become her donor. We weren't. Prayers continued from people all over the country— people who knew her and people who only heard about her through forwarded e-mails.

There'd never been a bone marrow donor drive in Lincoln, but a couple of Corinne and Bill's friends from high school decided to organize one. The Red Cross office in Omaha agreed to send a team if they were guaranteed thirty potential donors. Corinne's friends set out to get people there by asking the newspaper to publicize her story along with the information on how to register as a potential donor. The chances of actually finding a match for Corinne through this process were quite slim, but she was willing to allow her situation to be the public face for this campaign. This fit with her intention, and mine, that some good might come for others from her personal difficulties.

When the Red Cross workers arrived at the high school gymnasium in Lincoln, 250 people were lined up to greet them. When they ran out of supplies because no one had imagined such a turnout, a scientist in line went to his lab and brought back the needed items, so no one was turned away. A year later, we learned that one of Corinne's friends in line that day on her behalf became a successful donor for someone she didn't know on the national bone marrow list.

While this yearlong drama unfolded, I collected files of information on treatments not likely to be suggested by Corinne's medical team. Through my experiences with Ken, and as a social worker, I'd encountered "alternative" and "complementary" treatments, and I felt more open to that arena than my daughter.

"I'm much more conservative than you are, Mom," Corinne had told me when she was a young adult. I admitted at the time that that was probably true. Rose said, "That's a good thing. Since she needs to be different from you, you wouldn't want her to be more liberal than you are."

The files on my computer contained information forwarded to me on energetic medicine, nutritional supplements, faith healing, and so-called miracle cures. I was holding them until or in case I got an indication from Corinne that she might be open to explore something outside the Western medical model. Corinne's friends brought books and tapes to her as well, some related to keeping her spirits up while going through treatments and some related to the role of faith in healing.

Corinne was a devout Christian. She talked openly about how her personal relationship with Jesus informed all that she did. Some of the books people shared seemed helpful, while others seemed to me much too simplistic or encouraging of self-blame: "You weren't thinking positively enough if something negative came into your life." Or "This disease may be something you created to get you out of a bad marriage or a dull job." Fortunately, Corinne didn't fall for that kind of simpleminded thinking.

"I didn't need this disease to teach me gratitude for what God has given me. I love my husband. I love my job. I love my children, my family, and friends," Corinne would say.

Sometimes our different religious orientations created some

uncomfortable moments for me. Once, in Houston, a woman from a local mega-evangelical Christian church stopped by Corinne's hospital room. Corinne had gone for some testing, so while she waited, the woman engaged me in some small talk and then looked at me directly and asked, "Have you accepted Jesus as your Lord and Savior?"

"My daughter has," I told her. "Jesus is the center of her life. Me? I'm closer to his mother."

>>> ■ <<<

One Sunday morning, while Corinne was awaiting a bone marrow donor, my friend Mary Jane woke me with an early phone call and the instruction, "Get on the Internet and type in 'John of God.' I had a dream last night about you and Corinne," Mary Jane said, "and I woke up with the message, 'You and Corinne must go and see John of God.'"

Doing as Mary Jane suggested, I learned that John of God is a Brazilian healer who works closely with Western doctors to bring together the spiritual aspects of healing and the physicians' scientific skills. I was intrigued. I wondered if this could offer some way to bring the scientific world and Corinne's and my faith perspectives together. In the language of my dream, I knew we would be playing at a different table, perhaps the "Wisdom of the Ancestors" table. But what I really wanted was an opportunity to play at both tables at once. In my view, each of the systems of healing offered something I found missing in the other.

PREPARATIONS FOR A HEALING

Continuing my research on John of God, I learned that he worked in the small village of Abadiana in central Brazil, thirty miles from the capital. According to the website, at the age of nine, the uneducated peasant now called John of God incorporated the spirit of Solomon into his body. This is the Solomon known in the Bible as a king of Israel and the son of David. Reportedly, Solomon healed people through John of God. He was in his late fifties when I was learning about him and had continued through the years to incorporate other entities that, through him, treated sick people. Pilgrims came to his village from all over Brazil—indeed, from all over the world.

He has no memory of what transpires when he is in his trance state, and he makes no claims of any personal achievement. God does the healing work through him, which is how he got his name. Though he's spent some time in jail for what sounded to me like the equivalent of practicing medicine without a license, he still lives a few miles from where he was born, and he is known for welcoming collaborations with Western physicians and journalists. One of the entities he incorporates is a physician who was president of a Brazilian medical school, honored for his role in the eradication of smallpox in that country.

From that first early Sunday morning web search, remarkable synchronicities began to occur. In checking it out, I learned of a well-respected neurosurgeon in my community who, in addition to his scientific studies in Western medicine, had been studying shamans and indigenous healers in several cultures for many years. He was currently traveling to Brazil on a regular basis to study with John of God, *and* he had gone to high school with my friend Carol's best friend. Carol put me in touch with her friend, who invited us to a presentation the physician was giving at the hospital about his shamanistic studies.

>>> ■ <<<

The occasion was an official Grand Rounds and the hospital auditorium was filled with blue- and white-coated staff members: interns, students, physicians, nurses, and technicians. Carol's friend told us this would be his first presentation to his medical community about his studies of indigenous healing and that he would probably appreciate having some supporters in the audience. Having worked myself in the narrow confines of universities, where there was little room for ideas outside of the Western medical model, I appreciated the courage it took to come out to colleagues as he was doing. My stomach felt jittery on his behalf as we took our seats.

The central message I got from the neurosurgeon's presentation was that there are two types of healing systems in the modern world: the Western scientific system and the ancient indigenous ones. Each of these systems has much to offer, but they have become too separated from one another and need to be brought back together for the benefit of patients everywhere. He drew parallels and connections between these two worlds by explaining what happens in the brain when drums, beating at a particular rhythm, create trance in the people who hear them. He compared that to what happens in the brain when people are administered certain scientifically developed drugs.

After his presentation I was introduced to the physician, and we spoke briefly about my daughter and her situation. I showed him a picture of her and her three children that I carried in my purse. Yes, he did take pictures of people to John of God on his visits there. And yes, he would be willing to take my daughter's picture—but only if *she* requested it.

"Here," he said, returning the picture to me as he began to leave. "This belongs to you."

Seeing his determination that the request must come from her, I asked if he would be willing to talk with Corinne by phone to answer her questions directly, and he said he would be happy to do that. He gave me directions for contacting his office to arrange that conversation.

My daughter was polite and respectful as I talked about all this with her. I gave her the address for the website that described John of God and his work. She was able to see pictures of the Casa where he performed his healings. Amidst candles and flowers and pictures of Jesus and Mary and the saints, the Casa and its courtyards looked similar to Roman Catholic churches in the United States that I had grown up in and where Corinne had spent her early years. We had each veered off in different directions from that tradition, but it was reassuring to me somehow to realize that Brazil is a Catholic country and that John of God is related to that tradition.

Most Brazilians believe that anyone who has ever lived in the world is still connected to it and to those of us still here. Just as Catholics pray to the saints for assistance with worldly difficulties, people in Brazil believe that ancestors and other deceased entities will help you if you ask. I was fairly sure Corinne's friends and family in Nebraska from various Protestant denominations would not share this view. Nor would they find the connection to Catholicism helpful in understanding why Corinne would give her picture to a neurosurgeon who was a stranger to her to take to a Brazilian healer they'd never heard of.

My growing up in a "mixed marriage" family set me up to understand that there are many roads to Ultimate Truths. Dad was an independent thinker who loved the questions. He grew up in a rural Protestant community, though I'm not sure he attended church very often, as his parents both died the year he was five. Mother was an Irish Catholic who would never think of missing Mass on Sunday or questioning anything any priest ever said. From this upbringing and other life experiences, I recognized that no one particular religious tradition holds the answer to all my longings, but I respect that most of them hold enduring truths.

I was careful not to pressure Corinne in any way, but I asked, "Would you be willing to talk to the physician, and perhaps he could answer your questions."

"That's the trouble; I don't know what questions to ask."

"When I think of someone who might experience a supernatural healing, you are one of the most likely candidates," I told her. "I'm saying this not because you're my daughter but because of your faith in Jesus. From what I remember of Jesus healing people in the Bible, he often said something like, 'Go in peace. Your faith has healed you.' And you have more faith than anyone I know."

"Well, that's just it," she said. "I want to be sure this wouldn't endanger my faith in any way."

"Wise people of all faiths know that there are some energies you don't want to take into your body or your life," I said, supporting her concern. "You do need to be sure that whatever energy this man is using, it's compatible with your faith."

I don't know all that transpired in Corinne's phone conversation with the surgeon, but after they talked, she agreed to allow me to give him her picture to take to John of God. Her brother, step-dad, and some of my women friends sent their pictures along as well. As a measure of how focused I was on Corinne, I don't remember if I sent my picture or not.

In slightly more than a month, we received the news that a bone marrow donor match had been found for Corinne. The timing was amazing, given the many steps in the process. People register to become donors by having a blood sample taken and lab work done to identify three of ten possible antigen markers for matching. This information is placed in a national registry that is then searched for base-level matches to the person needing a donation. Several potential donors are contacted and told that they *could* be a match and asked to go to a lab to give another blood sample that, when analyzed, will identify their complete ten-point signature. If they can't be reached, they've changed their minds, or something has happened to their own health status to make becoming a donor impossible, those potential matches are aborted and the searching begins anew. And if the match is only a four- or five-point match, the search continues.

Somehow, all these potential difficulties were overcome, and Corinne had a donor: A fifty-one-year-old man who was a perfect ten-point match. We didn't know at the time how rare that was, though it did register as a game-changing event. We received this news with a smorgasbord of extreme emotions. Mine were fear and dread. I wished I could protect my daughter from the pain and discomfort that would be coming along with whatever decision she made.

Until a suitable match is found, a bone marrow transplant is only a theoretical possibility. It can take some people years to find a match, if ever. But now a real decision needed to be made. After amazement and disbelief, Corinne's emotions went to anger. "I feel like I don't have any options," she told me.

"You have options," I told her. "You just don't have any that you like."

She agreed. "Behind door number one is this icky option, and behind door number two is another icky option."

The trouble with the bone marrow transplant option (besides being highly experimental as a treatment for breast cancer) was that Corinne would be required to move to Houston for three months. She would need to be treated on a daily basis at the clinic.

"I'm thinking about the children. If I only have a couple of years left with them, do I want to miss six months?"

"It won't be six months; more like three," I said. "Remember, they said you had to stay a minimum of one hundred days. And depending on how you're doing, if the kids aren't sick with colds or something contagious, they can visit us in Houston. We can get an apartment with space for them."

We met with the transplant doctor in a small office at the medical center, and he described details of the transplant process. "While in the hospital you will receive blood over a period of several hours, which contains the stem cells of your donor. You will be in the hospital for about two weeks and watched carefully for side effects. In the weeks and months following, you will receive anti-rejection medication daily to control the tendency for your immune system to react against the donated cells or for the donated cells to attack you. This is called GVH, graft versus host disease. We monitor this carefully, and if it occurs we have methods to bring things back into balance."

The doctor added, "Having an astronaut mentality is necessary. There is risk, and when something goes wrong, it goes terribly wrong. But it is not a last-ditch effort. You don't launch a shuttle that is in bad condition."

Certainly Corinne was in good condition. She was amazingly strong and healthy, except for having a breast cancer that was resistant to chemotherapy. But the image of the recent shuttle disaster made me question his choice of analogy. I hoped he meant that Corinne's chances of surviving the bone marrow treatment itself were very good. The second issue, whether the new immune system would be successful in eliminating the cancer from her body, remained to be seen. Bone marrow transplants had proven effective for blood cancers, but breast cancer was a new frontier. Since she had an unrelated donor, there was more risk (more chance of GVH), but an unrelated donor's immune system was also more likely to bring new ammunition to the fight.

After much prayer and discussion with friends and family, Corinne decided to move forward with the transplant. A bone marrow transplant was the only treatment that held the promise of eliminating the cancer completely and forever from her system, and this was her fondest desire. She did not want to live Wilma's life—a nine-year roller coaster of one kind of treatment or another. The fact that a perfect donor match was found so quickly seemed an answer to her prayers, a strong sign that this was what God wanted her to do.

Though supporting her decision, I told her, "I'm still praying that you will not have to do this. My prayer is a version of the one Jesus prayed in the garden before his arrest: 'If this cup could pass, please let it pass.'"

>>> ▪ <<<

Several weeks later, when the physician returned to Fort Worth from Brazil, he met Rich and me at our home to return the pictures and talk about next steps. He brought pictures of the Casa and herbs for the people whose photos he had shown to the healer. He pointed out the large black X on Corinne's photo that he said was put there personally by John of God. Hers was the only picture with such a mark, and the physician explained that this meant the healer felt he could be more helpful to her if he could see her in person.

Seeing the mark on her picture and hearing what it meant, I was simultaneously excited and disappointed. I told the physician that while he had been in Brazil, a donor with a ten-point match had been found, and Corinne had decided to pursue a bone marrow transplant. She needed to be in Houston receiving radiation treatments several times a day to prepare. The neurosurgeon looked at me with a wary smile and a gleam in his eye. "Well, you are her mother. If she agrees to it, as a blood relative, you could go on her behalf."

"How would that work," I asked, feeling my eyes crossing a bit in that moment.

"You would take an article of clothing belonging to your daughter and present that and yourself to the healer on her behalf."

Thoughts began whirling around in my head as I tried to make sense out of this different paradigm. Later I wrote in my journal:

The notion that healing can take place over long distances or through someone else is, on the one hand, difficult to grasp, but on the other hand, why not? I remember reading in a physics book that cells once joined, after they were separated, continued to affect and be affected by one another over long distances. The cells of my daughter's body came from my body. Maybe that would count for something in this situation.

>>> ■ <<<

Corinne handed me the red drawstring plastic bag I was to take to Brazil. Inside the bag: a pair of well-worn pajamas. I smiled when I saw the familiar plaid peeking through the bag's opening. They were lightweight flannel, a red plaid pattern with bits of green and blue, and white cuffs at the wrists and ankles. I knew these to be her favorite, most comfortable pajamas, and just seeing them triggered memories of the ski trip to Colorado, our visit to Lake Michigan, the beach at Corpus—some of the occasions I'd seen her wear them. Since, as I understood it, the healer wanted something permeated with her energy, I felt she had made the exact right choice.

And she had made the decision to allow me to go to Brazil on her behalf after much prayer and consultation with friends and family. We'd been in Houston when I saw Bill and Corinne sitting in conversation on the veranda outside the hotel. I could tell from their body language that they were discussing Brazil. I'd been careful that whole trip to give them lots of space and not interfere with what needed to be Corinne's decision. And she needed Bill's support to make it.

Watching that tableau, my heart ached for how hard it is to deal with differences of opinion and perspective, especially around religious issues. And these all come to the forefront in the face of a life-threatening illness and decisions about modes of healing. Bill and Corinne had a strong spiritual connection through their belief in Jesus Christ. But there were differences, too. I remembered Bill's minister telling Rich and me, at their wedding rehearsal dinner, "Corinne has adopted her husband's religious traditions, but I have encouraged her to stand up and be true to her own as well."

I am still not sure what he meant by that statement, but I have observed through the years that Bill's religious community, fifth-generation Germans from Russia on both sides, was much more homogeneous than Corinne's. She was a Catholic who converted to Protestantism as an adult, whose father converted to Catholicism after growing up Protestant, whose stepfather was Jewish, and whose mother meets in the piney woods with an eclectic and ecumenical group of women to pray for peace in the world and the strength to serve life.

As my daughter prepared for one of Western medicine's most challenging procedures, I obtained her permission and began preparing to set out on her behalf to a healer in a small village in central Brazil. Corinne and I both recognized that I was moving beyond the time and space of our familiar universe.

She described her reasoning: "I believe that all healing comes from God, and I believe that God will heal me. And it may not come in a way that I am expecting it, so I must be open to any and all avenues for God's gifts to come into my life." I'm certain this is what she told Bill and how she gained his support.

My way of explaining this journey to myself? I didn't know whether bone marrow transplants or indigenous healers or some combination of the two would be the answer for Corinne. The only thing I knew: I was willing to do anything, including traveling to the ends of the earth, to secure for my daughter a way to overcome this incredible threat to her young life. Though neither she nor I understood how taking her pajamas to the healer could contribute to her overcoming breast cancer, we both surrendered—she to God the Father and his son, Jesus; me to the Divine Mother and the Great Mystery, which has no name.

TO BRAZIL

I told myself this could be the "backpacking solo across Europe" adventure I missed in my youth. My inner voice didn't sound too convincing. But whatever hesitancies I felt, there wasn't time to ponder the options. I had to travel to Brazil within an immediate time frame to be back in the States for Corinne's bone marrow transplant. I was her caregiver, and the cancer center wouldn't do the transplant without someone willing to be with her in Houston twenty-four/seven for three months.

There had already been postponements: waiting first for a donor, then for a safe incubation period after her donor returned from traveling outside the country. It wouldn't work for him to bring back SARS or some other disease and give it to her along with some of his bone marrow. And my daughter needed to receive radiation twice a day for a couple of weeks to lessen the amount of cancer in her system, making it easier for the donated bone marrow to work its magic. I checked to be sure that the area in Brazil I was to visit wasn't on some kind of "no fly and return home zone" as far as diseases were concerned. It wouldn't do for me to bring home some exotic microbe for her baby immune system to have to deal with.

My trip became a solo adventure when several woman friends decided for various reasons not to go with me. Besides schedule conflicts in their personal lives, our country had just started a war in the Middle East, and one woman's husband didn't feel it was a good time to be out of the country. My husband needed to work since I'd given up my paying job the prior fall, when running a clinic, seeing clients, and traveling back and forth to Nebraska and Houston became way more than I could handle. I did what my daughter had done in her life. I pared down to only what was essential, and my daughter and her children trumped all other concerns. I'm sure I was strongly influenced by the phone call I got from Corinne after we learned that the chemotherapy for her breast cancer wasn't working and that the road ahead seemed longer than anyone had imagined.

"I want my mom," Corinne admitted to me in that phone call. Corinne had been fairly independent since birth, so I felt surprised by her honesty and proud of her humility in these circumstances. "Most women don't have a mom by the time they're going through stuff like this, but I do, and I want your help."

Neither of us imagined my help would include a trip to Brazil, but here I was, searching online for a guide who escorted small groups of people to John of God. I found a woman whose next trip would take place the exact weeks I needed to go. A former dancer who had lived on an Indian reservation and written books about healers, she seemed a sister I hadn't yet met. I needed shots and a visa. There wasn't time to trust the mail, so a woman from my spirituality group visited the Brazilian Consulate in Houston and obtained a visa on my behalf. Traveling on airline miles donated by my friend Carol, I was bringing Corinne's pajamas, her picture marked by the healer, and pictures from family and friends.

We already knew that Corinne's doctors didn't want her to take the Brazilian herbs. After the physician had returned from Brazil with herbs from John of God for Corinne to take, she and I had sat huddled in a small examining room at the cancer center with four members of her treatment team. I relied heavily on the reputation of the neurosurgeon who studied with John of God as I explained, "Dr. B said they are mostly the herb passionflower, which has anti-anxiety properties, and they're safe to take simultaneously with Western medications."

After a beat or two of silence, as every person in the room seemed to be holding their breath, the oncologist from Jordan said, "We've just jumped back a thousand years and crossed a wide cultural divide." The transplant doctor from Japan said, "When we're dealing with transplanting bone marrow, we are extra careful to control everything that we can control. And in this situation, we know that we *don't* know the manufacturing process used and what traces of other elements might be included in the mix."

The final comments from the team amounted to: "It's your decision, but we don't want too many cooks in the broth." So Corinne's decision, which I supported, was not to take the herbs.

Just before I left for Brazil, Corinne had a consult with a radiation oncologist, an expert on inflammatory breast cancer (IBC), an aggressive type of breast cancer we had just begun hearing about from some of the patients at MD Anderson. Sitting under the backdrop of her awards and framed degrees, the oncologist explained that a breast cancer could start out as another type and then become inflammatory. It was her opinion that this had happened in Corinne's case. "I'm still holding out for the possibility of surgery either before or after the bone marrow transplant, depending on what response we get from the treatments," she said.

Corinne and I didn't like hearing that she might still have to have surgery after the transplant. And we missed the fact that this physician was providing what would turn out to be the most accurate diagnosis for the type of breast cancer Corinne had. IBS is rare, (1–5 % of all breast cancers), fast growing and more likely found in younger women. Looking back, this would explain how early tests didn't spot her cancer and why the usual treatments didn't work.

On that day however, Corinne was holding out for a bone marrow transplant from an anonymous, unrelated fifty-one-year-old male donor to eliminate the cancer from her body forever.

As for me, I wrote in my journal:

I am trying to stay centered and not get hopeful or discouraged, but this is hard. Perhaps I just need to stay in a place of

certainty that God will heal Corinne. Even Corinne's special
cab driver friend Immanuel has that.

Corinne and Immanuel had met when he picked her up at the medical center after one particularly bad-news day that had left her in tears after a session with her doctors. Through tear-fogged eyes, she noticed his cab license. "Immanuel. Doesn't your name mean 'God is with you?'" With that opening, in the forty-five-minute ride to the airport, they learned of their shared connection through Christianity and their relationship with Jesus, central to both their lives. Immanuel, an immigrant from Nigeria, became one of Corinne's strongest supporters and cheerleaders; they became members of one another's family. He would take her and a friend to his African church in Houston. When I returned from out of town, Corinne described the ceremonial dancing and drumming. "You would have loved it, Mom. There were people in colorful tribal robes laying their hands on me for my healing. And, of course, I cried when they touched me."

Immanuel became our family's special driver. When he was driving me to the airport before my trip to Brazil, I told him of my upcoming trip to John of God and that I was going on behalf of Corinne. His dark eyes sparkled with excitement as he turned around at a stoplight to shake my hand. He told me the bone marrow transplant and the healer in Brazil would work miracles together. "God doesn't want M.D. Anderson to get all the credit! What the doctors can do is wonderful," he said, "but God will get the credit when Corinne is healed and she presents her story in churches about what God has done for her."

>>> ■ <<<

The trip itself had plenty of challenges. My baggage got caught in the X-ray machine, my shoes set off the alarm, and the energetic sprint to the gate in Miami made me grateful I'd kept dancing to stay in condition. I spoke with Corinne from the airport and heard the tiredness in her voice. The family had gone to a hotel with a pool to celebrate spring break, but she couldn't go in the water because it would wash off her radiation marks. After the rest of the family returned to Nebraska, five-year-old Tori stayed with her mother in Houston because she'd been crying a lot and following Corinne around. "She just wants her mom," Corinne said.

The customs process in São Paulo took ninety minutes, creating yet another physical fitness test sprinting to the new gate. Swiftly pushing my luggage through the terminal on a cart provided by the airport, I was captivated by the dresses of the Brazilian women, colorful and figure hugging. I remember thinking the women must have spray-painted the fabric on their bodies. I marveled at their lack of self-consciousness, dressing in such revealing attire. More than any other marker, this convinced me I had arrived in another country.

My guide, Josie, and seven other travelers from the United States met in Brazil's capital, Brasília. We traveled the thirty miles to the village in two small vans. Arriving at a one-story, 1950s-style adobe motel building, we were directed to separate, sparse, unadorned rooms. Mine contained a metal twin bed frame with a mattress, a single chair, a table, and a small lamp. An adjoining room contained a toilet, a sink, a shower nozzle, and floor drain in the center of the room. It took a while to get the hang of the technology, but once you let the water drip for a bit through the nozzle's heating coil, the shower temperature went from freezing to tepid. The view from the attached covered veranda was the most engaging aspect of the space: workmen hauling dirt using carts pulled by donkeys; a plethora of colorful flowers, shrubs, and the butterflies they drew; an occasional young man strolling by with a cell phone to his ear; and the dramatic panoramic sky.

Before supper on the first night, I went for a walk down a dirt road, drawn by the setting sun. I heard beautiful music coming from a hut with a small child playing in the open doorway. Even though the language was Portuguese, I recognized the song as "Ave Maria," and tears began welling up in my eyes. I wrote in my journal, "*Here on the eve of my son Ken's birthday, here in this spiritual place, a song of the prayer that came to me at his death."*

After a delicious supper of cooked and fresh vegetables, Josie gathered our group. She smudged the room with sage and sweetgrass like we did in my women's spirituality group in East Texas and passed a talking stick for each of us to take turns describing what had brought us there.

"Strange things are always happening to me. I see ghostlike figures," an elderly woman from San Francisco reported. "So I'm here to get some answers."

"I was here in December. The experience was so wonderful that when I arrived back in Denver, I began making immediate plans to return," a woman in her early thirties said.

A health care administrator accompanying his wife, who was a writer, described his motivation: "Seeing the peaceful look on my wife's face when she arrived back in Seattle, I decided I wanted some of what she had obviously gotten here."

A middle-aged woman from Palm Springs had read about John of God quite recently and made her arrangements just two weeks before. Two German men living in the United States had come together—one back for his fourth time, this time bringing his friend.

We were instructed to make two lists of what we were praying for, a long and a short one. Items from the longer list could be placed throughout the week in the Triangle, a three-dimensional wall structure representing the Holy Trinity. A copy of the shorter list would be given to Josie to translate into Portuguese before she accompanied each of us on our visits to John of God.

"Since you are here on your daughter's behalf, you will need to go through the process twice," Josie explained. "The first week you're here you will go through for yourself, the second week for your daughter." Hearing this instruction, I thought of the flight attendant's directions for applying oxygen masks: "First make certain your own mask is secure and then fasten the mask on your child."

When I told Josie that Corinne's doctors didn't want her to take the herbs, she said, "You could take them on her behalf. You can take back some of the water blessed by the healer, and that could work as well. The herbs and the water are just vehicles to carry the healing energy."

Dressed in the required white attire, after a breakfast of cereal, fruit, and maté (a local drink that replaces coffee), we walked the few blocks through the village to the Casa. The streets were quiet except for a few young men setting up stations to sell cloth and trinkets. On our return trip to the hotel, they would wave their arms and disdainfully taunt us, shouting, "Bushh, "Bushh, "Bushh," an obvious reference to President Bush, who was in office at the time. We would shake our heads and smile nervously, realizing it was no longer possible to be entirely removed from home or to travel far enough away to escape the actions of our country's leaders.

Walking through the gardens at the Casa, we entered a large anteroom open on several sides to the mild morning air. Seating was limited to a few chairs and benches along the sides of the room. Since our group arrived early, we secured the remaining few seats. I noticed a woman, very pregnant, leaning against the stucco wall covered with pictures of Jesus, Mary, and the saints. Seeing her discomfort, I offered her my place on the bench, thinking, "Corinne would definitely give up her seat if she were here. As her surrogate, I better do that as well."

After about a half hour, we first-timers were invited to form a line to go into "the current" to meet John of God. The current is a field of energy formed when twenty-five to fifty people have meditated together for an hour. And John of God does not begin to incorporate his entities until that field has been established. It is these spirits who, with God's help, actually do the healing. After our visit, we would become part of that chorus of people meditating, and my heart sank a bit when I realized the prevalence here of sitting meditation. I preferred moving meditations such as dancing, walking the labyrinth—even washing dishes. Once our line progressed into the first current room, the heat and humidity suggested that the challenge might be even greater than I had feared. I remembered the mindfulness meditation I did with Rose, but that had been in a temperature-controlled hospital room. I wished I'd practiced more sitting mediation before I came.

Our line progressed smoothly into the second current room, where the healer was seated. Each individual pilgrim's time with the healer was only a minute or two. I thought about our managed health care systems in the States and I imagined they would be envious of the extreme efficiency of the Casa's system. Josie accompanied me and read my requests in Portuguese to the healer. He scribbled something on a pad, said something in Portuguese, and handed the paper to me. Later, Josie explained it was a prescription for my herbs and that I was to have psychic surgery on Friday.

>>> ■ <<<

Josie provided opportunities for us to experience other types of healing sessions beyond the village. It was a bonus I hadn't expected, but most helpful. It provided a context for understanding Brazilian cultural views on health and healing.

The spirit painter we visited was a man in his fifties, a former business executive who had owned his own company before beginning to paint under the guidance of entities. The central figures in each of the spirit painter's more than 43,000 paintings were flowers. His explanation: "Flowers are a beautiful expression of life, often present at celebrations."

The colors he used had meaning: yellow representing strengthening (especially of the nervous system); green an overall general healing color (representing emotional balance); and purple an antiviral, antidepressant. So it goes: light blue, anti-hemorrhage; dark blue, calming, relieves pain; medium blue: a cure for insomnia.

He began the session with a prayer I recorded in my journal: "*The world is heavy with war. Connect with your Christ energy and you will be sheltered. Peace that is necessary comes from us.*"

Then, in an aside to us, he said, "Tonight we are going to experience several spirits who work constantly for our benefit. During the work, remember your friends and family."

"My guide loves Strauss waltzes," he added, "so I will be playing them while I paint."

He painted quickly without brushes, using his bare hands. *Dum, da, da,* dum, da, da, and the waltz continued to play. He took only a few minutes for each picture. *Dum, da, da,* dum da, da. His hands moved quickly through the moist acrylic paint he had squeezed directly out of the tube onto the paper. His whole body got involved as he smeared the swirling colors onto the canvas and images of flowers emerged. Taking my turn standing next to him as instructed, I meditated on my husband, who at this point in his life was severely sleep challenged. I pictured him roaming our house in the middle of the night, sometimes slumped on the leather sofa, remote control in hand, staring at a flickering television screen.

As the loud waltz rhythm pulsated through my body, I had trouble standing still. The waltz is my favorite dance, and I often quote Marian Chace, the founder of dance therapy, who took dance into psychiatric hospitals in the 1950s: "Waltzing cures everything."

We were told the pictures are often used as a focus for meditation, and the painter suggested that the best place to put the painting is near where you sleep. "At that time, you are more open to its influence." At the end of the evening, after many of the members of our group had taken turns standing next to the spirit painter as he painted on behalf of their friends and family, we each made a financial offering, the money going to a children's charity. The pictures were large, just under the dimensions of the suitcase I'd brought, which was how I got two of them home.

A couple weeks later, as I was unpacking my suitcase, Rich was lying across our bed. I propped the paintings up against a wall in our bedroom and chattered on about the colors and what they represented. Turning around, I was amazed to find him sound asleep on top of the bedspread.

BEYOND THE ENDS
OF THE EARTH

My favorite spot at the Casa was a large covered veranda over-looking beautiful green hills, with a view of horses grazing in a field of fall wildflowers. No matter the temperature anywhere else, in that place there always seemed to be a breeze. And when a storm came up, which happened many afternoons, it was the perfect place to observe the electric sky. Here was the place to read and write in my journal. Often I sat in a chair with my feet up on the ledge. I could hear the birds, the music from the crystal baths, and in early mornings the muffled sounds of the voices of volunteers in the kitchen, preparing the soup we all enjoyed together after the morning sessions.

This was the place where I tried to make sense of what I was experiencing of this multicultural, multidimensional world. My Catholic school upbringing helped me relate to some of the rituals and symbols. As icons and candlelight took me back to the time of elementary school, I remembered a pamphlet I had found in the vestibule of the church. It was part of a series written by a Jesuit priest, and the title contained its message, "Your God Is Too Small." I remember thinking even then, "If my concept or ideas of God can fit into my little brain, there must be a great deal I'm leaving out." Many years later I read where a Hubble scientist expressed this notion from his more scientific perspective: "The universe is not only stranger than we think, it's stranger than we *can* think."

Looking back, it seemed this insignificant event created in me an openness to views, beliefs, and practices that might seem beyond my understanding. "Your God Is Too Small" made sense to me then as a young kid, and it makes sense to me now.

Staying open to other views meant facing my own honestly. After a particularly difficult afternoon meditating in the current, I recognized that I had faith that God *could* heal Corinne, but I didn't know if he/ she *would*. Sitting on the veranda, I wrote in my journal:

> *God could have saved Jesus from the cross, or my son Ken from dying of AIDS, but he did not. I know that God gave me many gifts through my experiences with Ken—but my prayers for Ken could not keep him from his destiny.*

On this clear day, just as I finish this sentence, I hear a clap of thunder. It seemed an energy from a larger realm underlining the truth of what I have just written.

> *In the years since, I've come to appreciate the limitations of my own, or any single person's, individual perspective. My appreciation for what a group of people can come to understand together has grown and deepened. Our brains are too small to contain the Great Mystery, but sometimes we get closer to the longer, bigger view when we come together in community rituals, as they help us reach beyond the dimensions of a particular time and place.*

>>> ▨ <<<

I entered the gathering room at the Casa a little after 8:00 a.m., just after I'd placed slips of paper with the names of family members in the Triangle wall sculpture. I had breathed a deep sigh, and a strong sense of relief overcame me. It felt like I had given my loved ones over to God. I thought of all the votive candles my mother had us light in Catholic churches when I was a child. I always thought each candle represented a petition—something Mother wanted, like healing for my sister Mary Jane, who was close to death after surgery at a month old. I wondered now if rather than a petition, the candle ritual was for my mother a way of turning over her infant daughter to God.

Walking into the surgery room, I actually felt jealous of the gurneys I saw handicapped people lying on. They looked more inviting than the wooden benches where the rest of us would be sitting. A man asked us to close our eyes and raise our hands if we were between the ages of eighteen and fifty-two *and* if we wanted a visible surgery. The videos I'd seen of visible surgeries didn't seem to draw much blood, and the subjects didn't seem to be experiencing pain, but they were real surgeries with a knife and without anesthesia. I was grateful I didn't have to decide about this because I was past the age when an actual physical surgery would be allowed. My surgery would be psychic, but people at the Casa assured us there was no difference in the effectiveness of the procedures; both are healing and life changing. Both types of procedure involved the same restrictions afterward. No pork, no chili peppers, no alcohol, and no sex for forty days. If this was a second surgery, the restriction was eight days. A week after the surgery, you're instructed to go to sleep wearing white with a glass of water by your bed. You pray, in whatever way you pray, and ask that the sutures be removed.

I was one of about twenty-five pilgrims in the surgery room, all with our eyes closed when John of God entered. I heard him move through the benches and gurneys without any words. When he stood close to me, I felt sensations of an opening in my ears, which continued to happen even after he moved away. I noticed sensations in my gut, and I felt a bit queasy. My sit bones began to hurt, and I wondered if we would be there as long as we had been sitting in the current. Just then we were instructed to open our eyes. "Be sure and ground yourself before walking," the man's voice instructed us in English, and he repeated the message in several languages. We were ushered out the back door, where Josie met us and escorted us to the herb store and then to a taxi. Entering my room after the two-block taxi ride, I lay down on my bed and fell immediately into a deep sleep.

When I awoke, I realized how deep my relaxation had become. Sitting on the veranda outside my room, the colors in the garden appeared vivid and vibrant, with a special clarity around the edges of things. Steve, the hospital administrator who was also recovering from his psychic surgery, spoke to me from his neighboring porch. "We look like a couple of convalescents in a TB sanitarium," he joked.

"Yes, we haven't had a chance to really rest until now," I said. We reflected on how, at one point, the health care system actually prescribed rest as a pathway to recovering health.

I slept soundly again in the afternoon and awoke with the question "Do we need to be in some sort of relaxed state for the God energy to come through to us?" I remembered Rich and me early in our relationship, holding hands as we walked around a small lake in the spring of the year. We had nowhere special to be, nowhere we were headed. Just taking our time, smelling the scent of new grass, watching the gliding ducks, meandering under the dripping limbs of the willow trees surrounding the shore. Finally coming to rest on a wooden bench, we noticed the soft, tender energy coming through our hands. Ever since, all these thirty-plus years together, we've commented when this happens. "Your hands have that energy again," one of us says. Is that energy the peaceful Life Force streaming through us? Confirmation of a presence some people call God? Sometimes after I've been teaching or performing, I feel that energy in my hands, accompanied by a warmth and joy coming through me. Everyone and everything looks beautiful. I look and feel beautiful, even to myself. Like the Navajo song "Beauty before me, beauty behind, beauty above, and beauty below. Beauty surrounds me. All is beauty."

>>> ■ <<<

A challenge to that beauty and peace came with the rain. The heavy rain brought an invasion of small flying bugs that didn't seem to bother me until I lay down, and then they wouldn't leave me alone. Someone finally found a screen for my window, but many of the insects were small enough to fly right through its netting. A strong sewer stench developed in my room as well, and no one seemed to know where it was coming from or what to do about it. These developments definitely interfered with my getting a good night's sleep and provided a challenge to my mood. I became full of doubts about entities, energies, and people seeing auras. My rational left brain would raise questions such as, "What proof do you have for any of this?" "Are you sure you're not grasping at straws or being hypnotized into a false reality?" I wondered if I had incorporated Corinne's doubts, since I was her surrogate, but I decided that I had enough of my own and needed to claim these as belonging to me.

A couple days after the surgery, I was writing in my journal and noticed that my left knee was quite red. It didn't appear swollen and it didn't hurt, so I didn't think any more of it. But on our weekend trip to Brasília to visit churches and other sacred sites, I noticed this time: My right knee was beet red. I showed it to one of the women in our group and she said, "Did you ask the entity for help with your knees?"

"No, but I did ask to stay strong and flexible to be able to keep dancing my life to the end of my life. I guess healthy knees would be pretty important to do that."

I mentioned my red knees to Josie and she said, "The entities are working on you, and they want you to know it and recognize it." This did seem like dramatic evidence that helped squelch my doubts.

Another Brazilian holy site, the Temple of Good Will, was on our itinerary. A large building shaped like a giant tepee, the temple housed one of the largest crystals in the world, which hung into its center from its several-story cathedral ceiling. Brazilian crystals are world renowned for having the highest clarity, and this quality enhances their ability to project energy over distances. The temple walls contained long slender windows from top to bottom, and the granite floor displayed a black-and-gray spiral design. It was clear that it was a type of labyrinth, as we observed pilgrims walking the spiraling black line to the center, taking turns standing under the crystal, and then following the spiraling lines outward, ending at what was called the Throne of God. I followed the path behind Josie, feeling a spring in my step, as though dancing rather than simply walking. Completing the pattern and arriving at the Throne of God, I felt a strong impulse to kneel, but I also felt protective of my body on the hard granite. I thought, "With my new knees, perhaps I can take a chance on kneeling here." As I knelt down, an overwhelming feeling of surrender came over me. I realized, "I must trust God—I must trust in God's will being done. It will turn out for the higher good of all." At that exact moment, a thunderbolt crashed, some music started playing, and a torrent of rain came. Through the window behind the Throne of God I saw water gushing down the side of the building, creating a waterfall. I questioned the synchronicity of the visual and sound effects: "Am I in a movie or theater production where everything is choreographed and timed to the exact right moments?"

Seeing the torrential rain, Josie announced we were going to stay inside a while to meditate. While the music and the storm continued, I sat next to her. She pointed at the water streaming down behind the throne. Tears began streaming down my face, and Josie placed one of her hands over one of mine. I could feel her energy, that soft Life Force energy coming through her to me, and a feeling of calming peace comforted and enveloped me.

Returning to the Casa, Josie gathered our group. She said the entities had directed her to do what she called an energy pass with each of us.

"It felt like you already did one for me in the temple," I told her. When it was my turn, Josie said the Hail Mary in Portuguese and then leaned over and whispered to me, "Mother Mary wants you to know she sends you light and love. She is sending you rose petals above your head and showering them down around your shoulders." This brought tears to my eyes and reminded me again of the time of Ken's crossing, when the Hail Mary prayer had come to me.

Sharon, the professional writer in our group, read a published story she had written about a friend of hers who drew portraits of angels. Sharon's friend began seeing angels ten years before when she had a bone marrow transplant. I felt amazed at the synchronicity with my daughter, and I imagined someone playing a chime. *Ding!* The woman's brother had died five years before. Another chime. *Ding.* And when she was drifting half-asleep, in that space between the worlds, her brother came to her. She asked if he was her angel, and he said he could be. *Ding!* The story mentions her friend drawing a pregnant angel, pregnant with possibilities and promise. Since Corinne was pregnant when her brother Ken crossed, I heard another chime, another *ding!*

By this time, I felt completely overwhelmed by the many similarities to Corinne's story in Sharon's book: a bone marrow transplant, a brother who died five years before, pregnant angels. Tears welled up in me as I remembered a pregnant Corinne saying good-bye to her brother on his deathbed: "Take care of my babies."

>>> ■ <<<

The second week I was to visit John of God and go through the entire process again, this time on behalf of my daughter. While Josie and I were preparing, she asked, "Did Corinne want her pajamas back?"

"I don't know for sure. We hadn't talked about it. I guess I thought she might want to wear them in the hospital during her bone marrow transplant."

"Okay, then. Hold on to the pajamas. Don't take them out of the bag—just show them to him, and I'll ask him to bless them for her to wear in the hospital."

Together we approached John of God and as Josie began to speak, he interrupted her. He spoke several sentences in Portuguese, wrote out a prescription for herbs, and handed it to me. Then, suddenly, with an energy that nearly took my breath away, he grabbed the pajamas from the bag I was holding and threw them on the floor beside his chair. He said something to Josie, and she translated immediately. "He will work on your daughter right now. Be seated in this room with her picture."

I found a seat at the end of a bench facing the healer. The line of pilgrims waiting to approach him was long, and he seemed to be taking more time with these second-timers than he had with the first-time people. I joined thirty other people meditating, and we were there about an hour. I experienced none of the discomfort of the other room. I felt surrounded by a cushion of air that seemed to be holding me up. I felt my windpipe open and noticed sensations in my lungs. I saw my three grandchildren and felt their lightness and joy. I thought of Wilma and how she spoke of the images of the children inspiring her through the many sleepless nights of her battle with breast cancer.

Later, Josie filled in details about our visit to the healer: "He understood before I told him. He said he will continue to work on your daughter. He knows what she needs. You don't need any more surgery." Then she asked, "When did he give you the prescription for the herbs? Before he took the pajamas?"

When I answered yes, she said, "Then the herbs are for you."

Josie got permission for our group to be in the second current room all day the next day and to go to the waterfall before we left.

>>> ▩ <<<

The waterfall was on private land very near the Casa, surrounded by rich vegetation. The owners of the land allowed visitors as long as women and men came at different times, no food or drink was taken into the forest area, and people came in what Glenda calls "a sacred manner." We entering the grove singing a song Josie had taught us,

154

"Comu vie na na' Comu vie ma-my'o-shun," an Umbanda chant to First Mother. I noticed the site had been outfitted with wooden ramps and handrails for handicap accessibility. We wore bathing suits and carried towels, preparing to take turns standing under the waterfall, immersing ourselves in the small pool below.

After our song, we stood in silence. In the midst of the trees, flowers, and lush vegetation, I noted a simple brown butterfly with yellow-and-white markings engaging in a quaint solitary dance. He flitted around and between each woman in the group, landing first on a shoulder, then the top of a head, then resting on an elbow. Finally the butterfly came to rest on my left hand, which was poised on the railing as I waited my turn. The butterfly stayed quietly on the knuckle of my first finger, rhythmically fluttering its wings. Next it moved to the knuckle of my middle finger and then to my ring finger. Finally it landed on the outside of my fist, in the crook where my little finger connects to my palm.

Time stood still as I recognized that the butterfly's wings were fluttering to the rhythm of my breathing. Then I realized my breathing was synchronized with the chant, which was still playing in my head: "Comu vie na na' Comu vie ma-my'o-shun." I tried even in that moment to determine how much clock time was going by. This personal "blessing" of the butterfly went on for all the time it took for two of the women to take their turns under the waterfall. But this dance of the butterfly was outside of conventional time and space. I felt this illusive creature was delivering an enchanting message of loving reassurance to me. My heart filled with a sense of wonder at this connection to another of "my relations."

My second time in the inner current room with John of God felt delicious. The healer came alongside the bench I was sitting on, and I heard him "incorporate," allowing another entity to enter his body—the entity that would do the healing. His breathing pattern altered clearly and dramatically, very like a person in the final stages of dying. Several times during the session I got an image of Richard and a sensation of a shooting pain over my heart. Throughout the session I experienced overwhelming love that seemed to fill every pore of my body.

Reflecting on this afterward, I realized that experiencing the Life Force energy as love simplifies everything. Nothing else matters and all else fades away. I thought of something I'd read in a book about healing that Josie had lent me. I had quoted from it in my journal: "*It is not the disease or infirmity that is healed but the person. Healing means connecting with the perfection of the universe called (by the words) God, Source, Love, or Light.*" Now looking back, if that's true, then although I came on behalf of my daughter Corinne, I definitely had a healing of my very own.

For our last visit to John of God, Josie taught us to say thank-you in Portuguese, *oh-bree-gahadoo*, and to take his hand when we said it. I cannot attest to the accuracy of my pronunciation, but as I held his hand in mine, I felt captivated by the essence of compassion streaming from his eyes. After a beat or two, with his other hand, he waved me abruptly on my way. I felt jolted by the powerful, nearly simultaneous contrast: his look so warm and loving, his arm gesture regal and dismissive.

In all the years since, I've not known what to make of this incident. It was definitely a demonstration of one way to let go. Like a warrior king wielding a sharp sword, he severed our connection and directed me to go on with my life. I have always preferred gentler transitions, but life has taught me that sometimes the only way to let go is to just do it. It's made easier when the other person is not still hanging on.

EXTREMELY HIGH-TECH MEDICINE

We'd taken to naming our summers. The first summer after Corinne's breast cancer diagnosis, she was taking chemotherapy every three weeks. In the rhythm and pattern so familiar to cancer patients in treatment, the first week she went from bed to bathroom to couch and then repeated the dance. The second week she might make it to a Little League ballgame or a school program but then be totally wiped out because every action required lots of rest to recover. By the third week she would begin to feel almost "normal" and then have to start the process all over.

Corinne loved being a mom. She loved being able to arrange her summer work schedule at the physical therapy clinic to have time for trips to the swimming pool and library, for bike rides on the trails, for craft projects at the dining room table. But that summer, family, neighbors, and friends helped out, and the children were asked to do more for themselves. Instead of Mom doing most everything for the children, the kids, who were ten, eight, and four, learned to make their own beds, pick up dirty clothes, set the table, and put dishes in the sink. We called that first summer the Summer of Self-Sufficiency.

The following summer, the summer of her bone marrow transplant, became the Summer of Sanitation. The children had to learn about germs and how they are carried and transferred and how to prevent that from happening. They practiced washing their hands thoroughly and often. They learned to time their soaping and rinsing by singing a few lines of a song, "Happy Birthday to You" or "Mary Had a Little Lamb" (one verse of almost any song works). We all developed the practice of coughing into the crook of our elbows and using antibacterial gel that we carried in our pockets. All this, and helping keep kitchen and bathroom surfaces clean, became the kids' part in protecting their mom and themselves from getting sick. They came to understand the need for these special precautions because of the immune suppression drugs she would be taking and the fact that her new "baby" immune system would be just developing its ability to recognize the intruders that cause infection. An extra incentive: they couldn't visit their mom in Houston if they were sick.

>>> ■ <<<

I'd been back from Brazil only a few days when I met Corinne in Houston for the last tests before her bone marrow transplant. She seemed as glad to see me as I was to see her. I wanted so much to share with her the deep peace I'd found at the Casa, even though I had no idea how I would do that. We talked intermittently over dinner, and then at the hotel, she shared her worries with me.

"The chemo I took in Nebraska works for everybody else. I keep asking why it didn't work for me. What am I doing wrong? Now I'm afraid the radiation won't work. Then I'll be out of options, unable to live and raise my children."

"Corinne, what do you feel when you go deep inside?" I asked.

"I had always felt I would be okay—that I would live. But I've stopped believing that voice inside."

"Why is that?"

"Once, when I was a teenager and I was crying about your and Dad's relationship, your friend Maggie asked me what I believed inside. I said I believed you would not get divorced."

Looking into her large blue eyes and beautiful freckled face, I saw the thirteen-year-old girl I'd called into my bedroom to tell that her father and I were getting a divorce. She didn't seem surprised, and though my sorrow hung in the air between us, she didn't cry. "I've cried a thousand nights," she said. "I don't have any tears left."

Corinne had been the first to speak out loud one of the difficulties in her dad's and my relationship. "Since we moved to Nebraska, Dad has been getting sadder and sadder, and you've been getting happier and happier." She had not made the connection I had between her dad's depression and his drinking, but she had seen us moving in different directions. Her father did not see the connection either. His opinion was, if I would quit mentioning his drinking, there wouldn't be a problem.

Before making the divorce decision, I'd driven to Utah to meet with one of my mentors, Barry Stevens, who wrote, *Don't Push the River: It Flows by Itself*. Several years before, I'd been drawn to her because this was a truth I needed to adopt. I told Barry I'd come to the place where I knew ending the marriage would be best for me, but I was afraid of hurting my children.

"That's impossible," she said in the tone of an elder woman who doesn't need to soften her opinions. "If you do what's truly right for you, it will turn out to be right for everyone else."

I sighed with a sense of relief from the burden I'd been carrying. I thought, "I hope she's right."

The divorce, the hardest thing I'd ever done to that point in my life, did turn out to be best for everyone involved. But Corinne had expected me to fix the marriage, and she was intermittently mad at me throughout her teen years and into her twenties because I didn't.

>>> ▪ <<<

During the period of the final tests before the transplant, one of the doctors decided to biopsy the rash that had been on Corinne's skin for some time. The report confirmed the rash was the breast cancer traveling around her skin through the circulatory and lymph systems. It was now on her other breast.

This news was devastating. Another disastrous development in a long series of what cartoonists represent as haywire and cussing symbols: "@#*%X!" Here was something else we'd never heard of, something else that set Corinne's disease apart from other cases of breast cancer. She was immediately concerned that this meant they wouldn't do the bone marrow transplant. She put a call in to the bone marrow doctor, but we couldn't bear to sit around waiting to hear back from him. As a mother and grandmother, we could always think of something to do for the children, so I drove us in my car to Target to get Easter baskets and treats to fill them.

Driving through midday Houston traffic, I thought of my time in Brazil and something Josie had told us before we left: "Each of you will have an entity assigned to you as your case manager, and he/she will go back with you. When you need their help, all you have to do is call on them."

"Okay, Case Manager," I said, half-out loud, "this would be a great time for you to manage some encouragement." The instant I completed the thought, my phone rang. It was my friend Cynthia from California, a powerful sign that I was not alone in the universe.

Later, when I called Cynthia back, her advice was most helpful. "Don't hold on to the suffering, the pain," she said. "Also don't hold the concept in your body/mind." This fit with advice I remembered getting from the nuns at school: "Offer it up. Give it to Jesus, Mary, or the saints."

As we pulled into the store parking lot, Corinne's phone rang, her bone marrow doctor returning her call. He'd gotten results of the biopsy and was not at all surprised by the results. "It's breast cancer. We knew you had breast cancer." So no, this would not affect his plans for a bone marrow transplant. But he did want to get to it as soon as possible.

It was decided that Bill would stay with Corinne in Houston during most of her two-week hospital stay for the bone marrow transplant. The plan was for we three grandparents—George, Bill's dad, Don, and I—to take care of the three children in Nebraska. While waiting at the Lincoln Airport for George to pick me up, I began to get agitated. Corinne and Bill were leaving for Houston in less than an hour. I calmed myself by remembering, "I'm not married to George anymore." He was Mr. Laid Back and I was Ms. Easily Excited, not always a good combination. He finally arrived with a story of missing the airport exit and getting lost circling back. He said he didn't know when Corinne and Bill were leaving. "That's one way to stay relaxed," I thought.

We arrived at the house with just enough time for good-bye hugs. Fortunately, Corinne had left a detailed calendar of what was supposed to happen and a list of things for me to follow up on. Instructions were fastened on the corkboard of the computer desk next to the list of phone numbers of people involved in the complex system of transportation to and from sports practices, games, and play dates. A daily chores calendar hung on the kitchen wall with the children's assignments.

I was proud of my first major accomplishment, getting the webcam operational so the kids could see and talk to their mom in her hospital room. Once connected, the kids enjoyed seeing their parents in blue gloves and the nurse with a mask over her face. They laughed at their dad in his getup, dressed like he was about to perform surgery on the television show *ER*.

We saw the beginnings of Corinne's wall of prayer, which was something she had come up with while I was in Brazil. When Corinne learned she'd have to stay in the hospital in semi-isolation for two weeks, she wondered, "What will I do with myself for all that time?" She came up with the idea of asking the people who had been praying for her to send their pictures and prayer requests so she could pray for *them*. "This will keep me from focusing too much on myself," she told me.

The prayer wall grew daily as the mail arrived. As it turned out, many more people than we had realized were praying for her. The e-mails she'd been sending to inform friends and family of medical developments during her Houston trips, a way to have less time on the phone and more time with her family when she was home, became an electronic journal of both her medical and spiritual journeys. Her e-mails were inspiring for people, and they forwarded them to friends who didn't know her. Many of those people began praying for her, and many responded to her offer to pray for them by sending their pictures.

Staff who entered the room asked questions about the many portraits and snapshots gracing her wall. A hospital chaplain heard about the wall and asked to interview her for the hospital newsletter. He often wrote about the ways patients coped with the stress of being in the hospital, and he thought this was something unique and worth sharing.

As the number of pictures grew, I began to recognize that my daughter's energy and influence were growing way beyond the confines of our family and her small community. By the end of her two-week hospital stay, the wall had grown to fifty or so pictures, enough to fill the two large poster frames I'd bought to transfer the wall to the apartment when she was discharged. She told me later, "I asked God to use me, to use me for His greater purposes." It was clear her prayer was being answered. She was being used beyond anything my protective mother instincts would have selected for her.

Years later, I read about a principle in Zen: "Generosity is the antidote to fear." I thought of Corinne's prayer wall and how she had focused on others in the midst of her own challenges and how that became a gift to her as well.

>>> ■ <<<

The day of the bone marrow transplant, Rich called from Houston at 9:15 a.m. to say they'd started the blood transfusion with the donor's marrow in it. I tried distracting myself with computer work and became distraught trying to get the printer to work. I finally recognized this as a kind of vigil, lit a candle, and did some meditation.

Corinne had asked me to have the kids write thank-you notes to her donor, so that became the project for the afternoon. The children knew we weren't allowed to contact the donor directly, but our thank-you notes would be given to him through someone at the hospital who had contact with a person at his end.

"Thank you so much for helping my Mommy get well," they printed carefully on the note cards. And Ethan, who knew a bit more about how the bone marrow is taken, (usually from the donor's hip, causing some temporary soreness) wrote, "I hope you feel better soon in the place where you gave my Mommy some of your bone marrow."

"I've had a sleeping, sick day." Corinne said when I talked to her that evening. I read her the thank-you notes the kids had written to her donor, and it seemed to cheer her.

Before joining Corinne in Houston as her caregiver, switching places with my son-in-law Bill, I needed to make a presentation in Austin at the 2003 Spirituality and Social Work Conference. One of Corinne's friends took my place with the grandkids in Nebraska, and I flew home to Fort Worth and then drove to Austin. Besides my own presentation, I was most drawn to an opportunity to walk the labyrinth, an ancient moving meditation with roots in many cultures. The conference was held in a university student center, so a canvas labyrinth had been laid down over a large gym floor. A few candles and some flower arrangements transformed the utilitarian gymnasium into a contemporary chapel-like environment. I walked silently at my own pace, crisscrossing a few other people as we each slowly traversed the spiraling pathway. Stepping into the center of the labyrinth, I said, "I surrender my daughter, Corinne, into the hands of God."

Reversing directions on the pathway, I continued walking in silence until I came to the end of the labyrinth. Stepping off the edge of the cloth onto the polished wood floor, a voice from deep inside surprised me with the message, "*We* are the hands of God."

Tears came to my eyes at that time, and still do as I remember that profound message and all the hands of all the people who helped us during that time and since.

BONE MARROW SUMMER

After a three-hour drive from Austin to Houston, I found the hospital and the transplant floor and arrived in the staging area outside Corinne's room. While outfitting myself with the required mask and gloves, I read the directions for visitors: "Keep gloves on if touching patient. Keep mask and gloves on for 15 minutes after entering the room. By then, the filtering system will have taken care of whatever you might have brought in."

I gave Corinne a hug, and after a few minutes of our catching up, I fell asleep in the chair next to her bed. When I woke up, I walked with her as she walked the circuit of the hospital floor, pushing her infusion pole, dressed in her mask and gloves. As a physical therapist, she knew the value of exercise and was determined to walk the circuit several times a day. As her dancing social worker mother, I was determined to keep up with her. In between walks and naps, I read literature and signs posted in the hall about the procedures for keeping potential infection away from my daughter. Fresh flowers were not allowed anywhere on the floor. Patients were to have no fresh fruits and vegetables for the next one hundred days. When moving about the hospital and eventually the city, Corinne would have to wear a mask and gloves at all times.

In spite of my studies, I managed to commit a major error the first week. One of Corinne's Houston friends, a former transplant patient herself, read in Corinne's e-mail that I had brought her some TCBY yogurt to the hospital. "You aren't supposed to have anything from a machine like soft yogurt, because you don't know what the machine has been cleaned with," she told me. This gave me quick notice that this post-transplant caregiving was going to be even harder than it looked.

After Corinne's discharge, we moved into the hotel until our apartment was ready. Bill came from Nebraska to help us move, and I picked him up at the Houston Airport.

"Ah, the Beverly Hillbillies," he said as he got in my car. This was a reference to the furniture on the roof, which I'd brought from Fort Worth. I agreed that we did look like the folks from the 1960s television series. But since we were planning to bring the children from Nebraska for visits with their mother, and the furnished places on the hospital social worker's list didn't allow children, we had to find our own apartment and furnish it. We settled on a two-bedroom place not far from the medical center in a large complex with a couple of swimming pools, exercise facilities, and walking paths.

Between what I was able to bring from home and what we borrowed from friends in Houston, we only had to rent mattresses, a sofa, and a couple of dressers. Corinne's favorite colors were blue and yellow, so that became our decorating scheme. Dishes and other supplies were secured from garage sales or department stores using coupons from the newspaper. Rich and I had decided to help Corinne make the most of the time with her children, including spending it in the most beautiful and comfortable environment we could afford to create.

While Bill packed up our hotel room for the move to the apartment, Corinne and I worked out on the hotel treadmills. Even though it was less than a month after the transplant, it was a rare day that physical therapist Corinne didn't exercise, and I accompanied her for most of it. On moving day, Corinne was able to give herself her infusion therapy at home, so while the medicine pumped through her, she and I unpacked boxes at the apartment, and Bill disinfected the kitchen and bathrooms to a standard that would be envied by any regulatory health agency.

After dinner out and a trip to the grocery store, Corinne was wiped out. I looked for the water blessed by John of God that I'd brought back from Brazil, but it had gotten discarded in the move. I felt extremely disappointed when I remembered how Josie had described the water as a vehicle to carry the healing energy. Later Corinne asked me to rub her feet, and I realized *I* could be a vehicle for that energy, or at least do something to help her feel better.

Handling the setup details for the apartment, like getting the phone connected, became especially difficult because we needed to be at the hospital a great part of every day. The apartment complex needed me to fax Corinne's written permission, but the fax number they gave me didn't work. My cell phone went out just as I tried to give the workmen directions. And returning to the complex, we found a complicated note in the mailbox asking us to list everyone who would be getting mail at this address, otherwise they would consider the unit unoccupied. We saw the mail carrier, and Corinne gave the note to her directly. Checking the mailbox later that day, we found another form and a note: "Please fill this out again, the wind blew the other one away."

"After this is all over and I'm healed, people will ask me to speak of my experiences," Corinne said, "and I'm getting enough material to create my own *Seinfeld* comedy routine."

>>> ■ <<<

We often needed to fill time between doctor appointments and treatments, so we explored small shops for something that might be considered a treasure. Although Houston is a shopping mecca of the free world, we were not often enticed to actually purchase anything. The only true desire either of us had was for Corinne to return to a cancer-free life and raise her children. Nothing else really mattered.

But one day when we were eating lunch at a small restaurant north of the medical center, an antiques shop across the street began placing furniture outside on the sidewalk. We felt drawn to explore its warehouse space, and Corinne soon became captivated by a lamp with a Tiffany-style glass shade of large yellow flowers. She didn't buy the lamp right away; she waited to show it to Bill when he visited. With his encouragement, the lamp became the first keepsake item for our Houston apartment.

When Tori visited the new apartment, it became for her a giant playhouse. She danced in the open spaces and crawled carefully through the tiniest crevices. She played quietly by herself, being careful not to make noise, since she understood that in an apartment building, your neighbors are close at hand. Suddenly, from the other room I heard a crash. I knew Corinne's beautiful lamp was in pieces on the carpeted floor.

Tori had crawled under the skirted table on which the lamp was sitting. When she tried to exit her secret hiding space, her foot got tangled in the tablecloth, pulling the lamp to the floor, bending the frame, and breaking a hole in the stained-glass shade. Corinne followed me into the room in time to catch me scolding Tori in a harsh voice. She attempted to calm me down, but her concern was for her little girl. She took Tori into her arms and, sitting on the floor, rocked and comforted her as Tori wept from fear and shame.

Corinne saw immediately that it was only a lamp and that her daughter was the one wounded. Initially, I had seen only the broken lamp, the symbol of all the bad breaks Corinne had been getting in her attempts to heal her cancer and go on with her life. Even as the scene was unfolding, I felt like the wickedest grandmother and the witchiest mother ever. Tori made a mistake, a miscalculation, and I made a worse one in how I responded to her. After a few minutes, I calmed down and apologized to both of them. My next trip home to Fort Worth, I took the lamp with me and found a place to get it repaired. Unlike all the mistakes and miscalculations it stood for, it could be repaired quite easily, and it became nearly as good as new.

A steady stream of visitors came to Houston. Corinne could not be left alone, so her sorority sisters from around the country and friends from Lincoln took turns flying in to spend weekends with her. This gave me a break from mothering, and Corinne a respite from too much of her mother. One evening when Corinne was driving guests to the airport and Ethan and I were following behind in my car with their luggage, my car had a flat tire. I had probably picked up a nail driving through one of the many airport construction zones, which were impossible to avoid. I called AAA, and although I'd been a member longer than most of their employees had been alive, that didn't help them find us. Our location wasn't showing up on their maps, and even the attendant they sent from a service station nearby failed to find us.

After an hour or so, I called on my case manager from Brazil for help. Almost instantaneously, a man from Australia stopped to help.

"My wife will laugh when I tell her why I'm late. She's always warning me I might get hit over the head playing the Good Samaritan," he said, looking around at me and Ethan and the woman in the car in front of us wearing a face mask and gloves. "You look pretty harmless," he said with a smile.

"That's my daughter in the mask," I explained, gesturing to her car. "She's thirty-five days past a bone marrow transplant, so I won't let her help change this tire even though she knows how to do it."

When my birthday came in the middle of July, my responsibilities as Corinne's caregiver left little time to think about how I might celebrate. That morning I dropped Corinne off at the hospital for her daily infusion therapy and left to grocery shop. When I returned, she presented me with a gift, and I was totally perplexed over how she had gotten it. My gift was a silver butterfly pin in honor of my special connection to butterflies, especially the one I'd told her about that bonded with me in Brazil. A young cancer patient's drawing had inspired the pin; Corinne had purchased it at the hospital gift shop. The nurse had switched her infusion pole to one with wheels, allowing Corinne to push it the mile or so across campus and back. Not surprisingly, this turned out to be my favorite piece of jewelry, reminding me always of the effort my daughter made to get it for me.

The big family event of the summer came the second week in August when all three grandkids were in Houston to celebrate Tori's sixth birthday. Kevin came from California to help out, and I was especially grateful because I had to be with Corinne at the hospital most days, and children weren't permitted near the transplant patient areas. Kevin was great with kids. As with his dogs, he always exercised just the right amount of discipline and fun. Seeing the fun they were having as he taught them gymnastic moves in the swimming pool, I remembered when Corinne first got sick, how protective she'd been of her brother.

"Don't come here," Corinne had told him. "I've got people helping me. What I want most is for you to get your career back on track." Kevin's back-and-forth travel to be with Ken through Ken's illness and eventual death had cost him his career momentum.

He didn't listen, and I couldn't blame him. He wanted whatever time he could have with each of his siblings, although he sometimes got mad at them for not doing what he thought they should do to get well. Unlike Corinne, and to some extent Ken, his faith was not in the medical establishment. He felt nutritional supplements to build the immune system were a better way to go than to inject poison into the body to kill cancer.

A few days after the kids arrived, William got sick. Corinne needed to avoid being around anyone who was sick because even a simple cold could be too much for her baby immune system to handle. So Will and I moved to the hotel to keep him away from his mother. When he complained of his jaw hurting, I took him to the minor emergency clinic nearby. Corinne's doctors were notified, and they asked the clinic to do a swab test, which it did, to be sure it wasn't strep. It wasn't. They also wanted the center's lab to keep the material from the swab for several days to see what developed. Their thinking was that ten-year-old William, basically a healthy kid, would eliminate the bug from his system in a few days. But should his mother, who had a compromised immune system, contract what he had, they would need a way to know quickly what it was in order to treat her.

The clinic would not do what I asked, no matter how hard I pleaded. They had their procedures! Years later, I found a quote by Yasutani Roshi that reminded me of this incident: "The fundamental delusion of humanity is to suppose that I am here and you are out there." Unfortunately, our health care models can't stretch wide enough to treat a whole family, even though in circumstances like this, we were clearly all in this together.

>>> ■ <<<

Bill and Rich came down to Houston for Tori's birthday, and with Kevin, the men took the kids bowling while Corinne and I exercised to a yoga tape at the apartment. It was good that we had that interlude of peace because the rest of the birthday was full of challenge. Although Will was feeling better, he and his mother still had to be kept separated, so Will sat at one end of the table and his mother at the other. Will had to wear a mask and gloves to prevent the spread of his germs to Corinne, and he wasn't a happy camper about that. He pouted and refused to have his picture taken when everyone else was posing for pictures. I convinced him with the following argument: "William, when you are grown up and have your own children, you will be telling them about this weird day when you had to wear a face mask and gloves to your sister's birthday party. And guess what—they won't believe you. That's when you'll need these pictures to prove you are telling the truth."

Tori had selected the Little Mermaid as her party theme, and although Corinne was not able to make her usual spectacularly decorated birthday cake, she did design a "pin the fin on the fish" game. I can still see Tori's blonde head bending over the table while her mother's gloved fingers put the pieces together. The final salve to William's bad mood came when we all agreed to wear face masks and gloves for a picture. Tori finished her birthday week by staying with me at the hotel the night before they left. She recognized that she wouldn't have another opportunity for a while. "I can't just ride my bicycle over here, you know," she said.

It took both Corinne and me, each driving a car, to get Bill and the kids, Kevin, and everyone's luggage to the airport. At the airport, the kids were hanging on to Corinne, having a lot of trouble saying good-bye. Observing the scene, a compassionate security guard wrote a pass for Corinne to accompany her children to their gate. When she returned, we said good-bye to Kevin, and I followed Corinne's car back to the apartment. She was driving slowly. I knew she was crying.

When we got back to the apartment, she had a lot to say about her brother Kevin and how he'd hurt her feelings with his judgments of how she was doing this cancer journey. His views of nutrition and alternative medicine ran counter to her medical choices. I had noticed Kevin's judgmental attitude during the visit and attempted to talk with him about it.

"I understand this is hard for you, Kevin. You have such a strong belief in your amino acids that you want to share them with her. But she's made different choices, and they may not be compatible with what you're suggesting. It isn't personal. She wasn't willing to take the vitamins I've taken for fifteen years when I offered them to her. I remind myself that I don't know what I would do in her situation. We can't know that until it would actually be happening to us."

Continuing to vent her frustration, Corinne said, "Kevin wanted me to visualize my future. He suggested I come and visit him in California. I told him, 'I'm visualizing being home with my family, Kevin.' He never asked me what I *do* visualize. How about seeing my six-year-old daughter graduate from high school?"

ONE HUNDRED
DAYS PLUS

My efforts to notify someone in authority at M.D. Anderson about the offensiveness of the "You Really Can Prevent Cancer" signs in the restrooms increased after a particularly unpleasant experience there. Corinne had finished a test where she had been given iodine intravenously, and while in the restroom, she began experiencing nausea and diarrhea. Her blood pressure dropped to the extent that she risked passing out when she tried to stand up. I asked a woman in the restroom to go for help while I stayed with my daughter. Standing over Corinne, holding a wet paper towel to her forehead, while we waited for emergency personnel to arrive, there it was, the offending sign shouting its insipid message: "You Really Can Prevent Cancer!"

Having been the director of a behavioral health clinic, I knew the importance of patient/family satisfaction questionnaires. Facilities are rated on their scores. I was sure, from the otherwise excellent treatment we were receiving from this world-class cancer center, that the administrators would want to know about the negative impact of the sign. I made sure my complaints were spelled out clearly and in detail, even onto the margins of the patient satisfaction forms. While waiting for a response from the Quality Assurance Department, I had a long conversation with the center librarian, expressing my distress. She listened respectfully and referred me to the department responsible for the sign. I followed up by visiting someone in the Cancer Prevention Department. I told the woman what we thought about this sign and added comments I'd heard from other women. She listened, seemed concerned, and promised to pass the information on to her boss.

As we visited the center and the women's rooms throughout the months, that blue-and-white "You Can Prevent Cancer" sign continued to taunt us as we washed our hands and pulled paper towels from the dispenser. Finally, I wrote an expressive and explosive letter to the president of the medical center. After dispelling the charge of my pent-up frustrations, I carefully edited my remarks, to avoid being placed immediately in the nutcase file, and sent it. I said, "Show your designs to real patients and family members before you engrave them into your system of care. You may well find such a practice worthwhile. We have our own unique wisdom and we would be glad to share it."

I got a letter back from the vice president, to whom my letter had been forwarded. His letter thanked me for calling attention to the offending sign, and he assured me that the signs would be taken down immediately. I remember feeling some small encouragement and sense of accomplishment. My daughter, whose treatment journey at that point had been going from bad to worse, read both my letter and the administrator's, shook her head, looked at me with both eyebrows raised, and said, "We'll see."

>>> ■ <<<

Eating in restaurants around Houston required us to take special precautions. Corinne had promised Bill she wouldn't use regular restaurant cutlery, since he had questions about how carefully it was washed. Rich had gone to a Costco and bought enough individually wrapped silverware for us to open our own restaurant, so we always carried our own. During one lunch out, Corinne began an unusual conversation.

"You know, Mom, when I mention to my friends that you teach InterPlay, they look at me kinda funny."

When I asked what she meant, she said, "The word sounds kinda sexual to them. You know, *inter*course, fore*play*."

I replayed the conversation over in my head that night instead of sleeping and wrote in my journal:

> *She's 41 years old, and I've been at her side whenever she has needed me for the past year and a half. We've been through tough and fun times together but I still embarrass her with her friends. I must always keep in mind, I am her mother. I am not her friend. And no matter how long we both live, I will never lose the ability to embarrass her.*

From the distance of many years, I feel sympathy for each of us—for Corinne for her wish that her mother could be more like other mothers, more like her, and for the mother I was then, longing to have my daughter be proud of me rather than embarrassed by my uniqueness. I'm grateful we were able to have this conversation, and if Corinne had lived to raise her own daughter, I'm fairly certain we would have come to a place of mutual understanding, as she would have had to grapple with the differences between them.

>>> ■ <<<

"We have to talk about the biopsy," Corinne's bone marrow doctor said when he visited her during her infusion therapy session. "The cancer has returned to the skin on the other breast. It isn't good news, but it's not time to panic. The oncologist is putting you on Zolada, a pill chemotherapy you were on previously without side effects. I could release the immune system, and it would take care of the cancer, but given you are a MUD, a case with a matched unrelated donor, I'm fairly sure you would get GVH. As you know, this is the balancing act with a transplant, keeping your new immune system from attacking you. I'd like thirty more days before we begin to reduce the medicine that suppresses the immune system."

After he left, Corinne was in a quiet, depressed mood. Rich called, but she didn't want to talk to him. I remembered the time in Brazil when Josie transferred the most peaceful energy to me through her touch. I stood at the foot of Corinne's bed, took hold of her feet, and imagined doing the same thing to her. It seemed to work. Later, when she became upset again, I touched her back as she lay on the bed. I was looking for anything that might ease her pain or help her deal with it, and I thought about praying. I felt a bit self-conscious doing it, but I began praying out loud for her.

"Father, Mother, God, thank you for all the help you have given us in the past. You have brought us through many difficulties. Hear our prayers—on behalf of this woman, your faithful servant, who has been courageous and determined, faithful and obedient in staying the course for her healing. Give her the strength to continue. Inspire her with hope and let her feel your love. I ask this in Jesus's name. Amen."

"Thank you, Mom," Corinne whispered.

At our next meeting, the bone marrow doctor said, "Everything is on schedule. In two weeks I will wean you off the medicine that is holding back the new immune system. It's okay to do yoga at the yoga center but not the hot yoga. It's okay to go to the conference that M.D. Anderson is sponsoring about living fully with cancer. Just wear a mask."

This all sounded like good news. We didn't want to take the hot yoga class anyway. Regular yoga classes and the conference—this meant we could have some normalcy in our lives. But then: "It could take several months for the immune system to go to work on the cancer," he said. "I want to stay on top of the cancer rash on your left breast."

"It looks like I'm going home with *anxiety*," Corinne said.

>>> ■ <<<

Toward the end of the summer, one of Corinne's sorority sisters took her vacation and came for a week. I went home to Fort Worth to teach an InterPlay workshop and then drove to Austin to teach another one. Since Corinne's friend needed to leave early Monday morning, I drove the three hours straight to Houston without stopping for dinner. The workshop had gone well, and I was in great spirits, driving through a light drizzle, singing much of the way.

I was pretty hungry when I arrived, so Corinne offered me some wonton soup she had in the refrigerator. While I was eating the soup, she showed me her swollen breasts and red body rash. It was graft versus host disease: her new immune system was attacking her.

She and the friend staying with her seemed to have gotten used to how she looked, but I was shocked and appalled. The soup had hardly reached my stomach when I went into the bathroom and threw it up. And I continued throwing up throughout the night and throughout the next day. Corinne's sorority sister left before dawn, and when things didn't improve for me, I realized I needed some medical help.

This created a special challenge, because Corinne couldn't be around me now that I was sick. I called a friend to come and help, but Corinne hadn't met the friend and didn't want someone around she didn't know. I found this to be especially annoying coming from the woman who made instant friendships with people she met on airplanes.

I agreed to let Corinne drive me to the minor emergency clinic, only a few blocks away, but I insisted she not come in; no telling the myriad diseases lurking in a medical waiting room. After a half hour, I was taken to a small room and given fluids intravenously. When they handed me the bill for $3,000, I was almost as upset as I'd been when they refused to culture the swab from William's sore throat. My own physician later concurred with the treatment, although not necessarily the price. The vomiting was a result of my having become dehydrated, so I definitely needed fluids. At another level, my physician and I both agreed, I was attempting to purge myself of what I could no longer stomach.

>>> ■ <<<

Day one hundred since the bone marrow transplant finally arrived. Now Corinne could return to her family in Nebraska. I awoke to the aroma of the coffee cake she was baking in our apartment, a little taste of Nebraska as a thank-you to the nurses and hospital staff. I felt a tinge of mother-guilt that I hadn't done more for those nurses and aides, whose kindness and care she'd relied on these past months. Next I heard the smoke alarm going off and Bill teasing Corinne that she'd better not set off the apartment's interior sprinkler system.

At the hospital, Bill was cheerful and in a talkative mood, standing beside Corinne's bed. He was telling stories of the kids while Corinne got hooked up to her fluids. The doctor, who had been out of town the prior week, entered the room followed by his entourage of interns and other staff.

In the presence of three additional doctors and a nurse, Corinne's doctor asked her to recount the events of the past week—the rash and the swelling of the breasts.

"It all happened pretty much together."

"How big did you get?" the doctor asked.

"Dolly Parton–size." Finally, she lifted up her shirt. "Well, let me flash you." She showed with her hands the size her breast had swelled to. The nurse, who had seen her the prior week, leaned forward for a better look, then nodded her head in agreement.

The doctor asked to be excused to confer with the team, which was unusual.

"Now you guys are scaring me," Corinne said.

The doctor smiled and explained, "It's just that I felt you would be more comfortable not having to listen to our discussion."

He left the room with the medical team following behind, and when they returned in a few minutes, he asked Corinne, "What do *you* think? What do you want to do?"

But Corinne didn't want to speak first. "What do *you* recommend?"

"I'd like to keep you another week. I want to be very conservative, to be sure the GVH isn't going to become a bigger issue. Right now, it's good. The topical cream is controlling it without having to take anything orally."

He wanted to keep her on the intravenous fluids every other day until he saw her the next Tuesday. He put her on a different antibiotic to be sure her low-grade fever wasn't due to infection. And he took her off the oral chemo.

"What happens with the cancer in the other breast if he takes her off chemo?" I thought, but I didn't say anything.

Corinne was disappointed but resigned to waiting another week to go home. "I don't trust the hospitals in Lincoln to know how to handle a post–bone marrow transplant case."

As the mother, I was even more conservative than the doctor. I finally admitted out loud, "I'm relieved."

Years later, I found a report on the cause of the *Columbia* shuttle disaster, which for me always seemed connected to our experience of Extremely High-Tech Medicine in Houston during that Bone Marrow Transplant Summer. As spectacular as the shuttle's scientific achievements had been, the culprit was a small piece of Styrofoam insulation that had fallen off the shuttle during its takeoff from Earth. This was not an uncommon occurrence, having happened multiple times during other shuttle liftoffs. But this time, the location, speed, and force of the event created a hole in the left wing the size of a soccer ball. Most amazing to me was that the scientists did not anticipate that the tremendous speed at liftoff could propel even this small, lightweight object with the force of an explosion—creating a gaping hole in the container and therefore sealing its tragic fate.

Nobody had any idea that the hole in the shuttle was *that* big.

Nobody had any idea that Corinne's breast cancer would progress *that* quickly.

DANCING ON THE EDGE

The following fall in Nebraska, Corinne's time was spent with all that's involved in being a mom. Laundry and meals, attending the children's sporting events, walking Tori to school, participating in a play the children put together for family members at Thanksgiving. And she attempted, without much success, to have the family piano repaired. The upright piano she'd played as a child, which had belonged to her father's mother and which her children used for their piano lessons, had been declared "beyond repair." I'm not sure what's involved in such a diagnosis, but it had something to do with the piano's inability to retain its tuning.

She visited a music store in downtown Lincoln and mentioned to a friend the beautiful baby grand piano she'd seen there. It would fit perfectly in the front alcove of the bay window in their living room. The previous owners had had just such a piano in that very spot. But this was an "I'm just looking, thank you" trip, since a new piano was out of the question for a family budget already stretched by health insurance co-pays and airline tickets to Houston.

Soon December came and with it Corinne's three-month, post–bone marrow transplant checkup in Houston. Corinne and Bill had hoped to be back to Nebraska within a week to get ready for Christmas, but they were forced to remain in Houston for several weeks beyond what they'd expected. They spent their eighteenth wedding anniversary in a hospital room and received the devastating news that the breast cancer was out-pacing the new immune system. They arrived back in Nebraska after dark on Christmas Eve and, approaching their street's cul-de-sac, were stunned to find their conservative two-story gray colonial home trans-formed into a flashing, blinking duplicate of Chevy Chase's Griswold house in the movie *National Lampoon's Christmas Vacation.* Lights of all varieties outlined every arch, soffit, and architectural feature of the house, including the shrubs and trees. Friends and neighbors had donated lights from their own collections and spent an entire day on ladders construct-ing this illuminated "Welcome Home" monstrosity.

Yet an even more gigantic surprise was in store. Corinne had asked Rich and me not to come for Christmas morning but to wait until the evening. "You know how crazy Christmas morning always is, and with us having been gone so long, it'll be even worse."

"You don't even know the half of it," I thought.

Quite a few friends stopped by Christmas morning, which was somewhat unusual since they weren't home with their own families. But several friends had done Corinne's Christmas shopping for her, so that was a good excuse to report in and wish the family a Merry Christmas. Ethan told me later, "After the people were there about a half hour, I saw a truck from the music store pull up in our driveway. I thought they must be coming to pick up our old piano. I opened the door, and there was a man carrying a piano bench."

Corinne's friend Susan, one of the head instigators, told me later that as the delivery man entered the house, he said to Corinne, "Where do you want this, lady? And don't say back on the truck."

As cameras flashed, Bill, Corinne, and their three children watched in amazement as a new baby grand piano was carefully placed in the living room alcove near the front window. More than forty co-con-spirators from around the country—people who found out about the family's need for a new piano through the e-mail networks of Corinne's friends—had signed the card that accompanied this extravagantly generous gift.

After three weeks in the hospital, Corinne needed to spend time resting in her bedroom on the second floor. The children would alternate playing the piano, and the music would waft up the stairs, a comforting balm to Corinne, like the scent of chocolate chip cookies or the aroma of an elegant floral bouquet. The music traveled up the curved staircase as a gift from whichever child was playing and from all the people who had made the piano possible. Without words, its rhythm and melody said, "We love you. We want you to get well."

When I got home to Fort Worth, I mentioned the story of the piano to my doctor, Mary Ann. She said, "In medicine, when a person gets well, the last person who touches the patient gets the credit. But some of us have been doing this long enough and are humble enough to admit, sometimes it's not anything *we* do. Sometimes it's the piano."

>>> ■ <<<

Some moments stay with you for a long time, perhaps your whole lifetime. Not that you dwell on them, but sometimes when you're relaxed, a snippet of the memory comes to the forefront. This happened recently when I had lain down to rest a bit before getting ready for an evening out with my husband. I closed my eyes and heard my daughter's voice, as I had years before in the hospital room, coming from behind me. "I'm gonna die," she said simply. It was a few weeks before Christmas, and on this occasion she had gotten the latest report on where the breast cancer had spread: to her pelvis and rib.

Looking back, I wonder, was that when we knew? When it was confirmed that the new immune system was having as much trouble dealing with her cancer as her own immune system had had? Was that the moment when Corinne's situation got separated from the 80 percent of women who suffer with breast cancer and survive it? It was one of the bleakest days of the whole treatment journey. Corinne said the words out loud, but there would be disbelief of that reality for eight more months. After the team of doctors and their entourage left her hospital room, I didn't know what to say to her. I gave her a hug and told her I was going to the hospital chapel to pray. I didn't add, "to pull myself together," but that was my strongest hope and intention.

I opened the chapel door expecting a faintly lit place for quiet meditation, but the room was bustling with people. An African American woman minister and several women singers were preparing for a lunchtime service, and the small room quickly filled with staff, patients, and visitors. As the service began and the praise choir began singing, I realized that quiet wasn't on the agenda and quickly adjusted my expectations. "Corinne loves Jesus, and I love to sing, so this could work out," I thought.

I soon recognized it is not possible to sing and cry at the same time. So I alternated. I would sing for a while, and then I would cry. I remembered a line from a folksong, "Singing is a way of weeping in the soul," and it reassured me that, through these songs, both my body and my soul were weeping for my daughter, her three young children, her husband, her father and stepfather, her brother, and myself.

At the end of the formal service, the minister invited those who wanted a special blessing to come forward. After observing other people for a few minutes to see how it was done, I approached the minister, who stood behind a railing, and knelt before her. I mumbled a few sentences about my situation through my tears. The minister interrupted me: "Your daughter has had a bone marrow transplant?" This shocked me, since that wasn't one of the things I'd said, and I wondered how she knew. Thousands of people were treated at the cancer center on a weekly basis, but only a handful of them have bone marrow transplants. And my daughter was among the first dozen women in the world to have a bone marrow transplant to treat breast cancer.

"Yes, and in spite of that, the cancer has spread."

The minister's expression changed dramatically. Her pupils shifted to the side of her eyes, and she said, "God tells me your daughter is already healed."

As I studied her face, I did not doubt her sincerity, but questions swirled around in my head. I wanted to believe that what she was saying was true. Checking in with my body, I felt a clearing and some relief from the pain I'd been carrying.

"Let us pray," the minister said, placing the palms of her hands on the sides of my face, over my ears, as I bowed my head. She prayed out loud for my daughter and me, and though her words are lost to me now, I can still feel the tremendous energy emanating from her palms. As she prayed, I cried, the energy from her hands pressing into my head, my skull feeling like it would explode. When she finished, I had the most incredible headache, but I thanked her as I dabbed at my wet face and blew my nose into a tissue.

I left the chapel and went for a brief walk around the hospital grounds, trying to make sense of all the conflicting information. Spiritual healers had always maintained that Corinne would be fine. Glenda had traveled to a woman's spirituality conference in Scotland the spring Corinne was first diagnosed. She consulted with several indigenous medicine women, who each gave the same opinion: "Corinne would be fine." John of God had told me, through an interpreter, that he "knew what she needed and he would continue to work on her." The X-rays and body scans showed a different picture. The Western physicians told a different story, though I reminded myself that the bone marrow doctor had not given up yet. The new immune system, being only seven months old, is still immature, and when it becomes fully mature, it could knock the cancer out.

When I returned to her hospital room, I described to Corinne what had happened in the chapel and repeated what the minister said: "God tells me your daughter is already healed."

Corinne smiled and her eyes softened as she said, in reference to the e-mails that she wrote to friends about her medical and spiritual journey, "Sounds like you have an e-mail of your own to write this week, Mom."

Looking back, this incident with the minister provided a lesson for me in the difference between a person being healed and a disease being cured. Of course, I wanted Corinne's disease to be cured, because that seemed the only way she could stay with us. But I was witness to the growth that she had made. I could see she had healed into a whole person, full of love and compassion for herself and others. And I could not deny the effect her healing presence was having on others. She was indeed being used, as she had prayed to be used, for God's own purposes.

>>> ■ <<<

"We're doing good, in the midst of The Big Suck," my husband would say when people asked how we were. Then we'd smile and shake our heads and feel grateful for how good we really were doing, under the circumstances. By the end of the first year of Corinne's treatment, we had given up holding our breath, waiting for the next shoe to drop. Whenever it did, it only seemed to double our trouble.

The Big Suck didn't go away. Rich's mother, Pearl, the head worrier in the Jewish wing of the family, was constantly amazed by the challenges that just kept coming for Corinne and by her unwavering faith in Jesus Christ.

"I envy her faith," Pearl would say, "but I don't understand it. I can't imagine how she stays so faithful."

Socrates's advice to his students to practice dying was incomprehensible to Pearl. She would say, "What a lousy system. You live, you struggle, you get sick, and then you die." She never mentioned what system she thought would work better, but she definitely disapproved of the one we all have to experience. One day, just after we'd gotten more bad news, I was talking on the phone with Pearl from our hotel room in Houston. She felt so bad about all that Corinne was going through, and on this day, her anger at the situation got the best of her.

"So *where* is her Jesus now?" she said, her anger erupting abruptly into my ear. From where I was seated in our hotel suite, I could see Corinne in the next room, sitting on her bed reading.

"I can't say about Jesus," I told her, "but right now Corinne is reading a book about Job. I think he's one of your guys."

The subject of Jesus came up another time, in a more subtle conversation with one of Corinne's friends. The friend had asked Corinne what she thought Jesus was doing in relation to her situation.

"I'm sure Jesus is crying too," Corinne said. "Prayers are always answered. It's just that sometimes the answer is no."

Like Pearl, I was not in the place of accepting no for an answer at that time. But Pearl surprised me one day by admitting that sometimes when she got upset, she would visit her husband Jack's crypt and she would talk to him about Corinne. "I don't know if there's anything after this life. I don't know whether he hears me or not, but I feel better when I leave."

>>> ▩ <<<

"When we think about someone and wish them well, that's praying," the minister from Corinne's church told me. It was now late spring, the year after the bone marrow transplant, and we were in the waiting room of the hospital in Lincoln, waiting for Corinne to come out of brain surgery. The breast cancer had gone to her brain before the new immune system could eliminate it, so the surgeons were removing a couple of small tumors to give the new immune system more time to do its work.

If that was right, that wishing someone well in your heart was a form of prayer, then I was praying unceasingly for my daughter, along with many, many other people. I had different methods of praying; one particularly unsophisticated method was just the word *help*. "Help me! Help our family!" I'd asked the Brazilian entities, particularly the one Josie called my caseworker. And when getting to sleep seemed impossible, I would join the Hail Mary prayer to a breathing exercise and repeat it like a version of the rosary repetitions I'd said in my youth.

But for me, the best kind of prayer has no words. Dancing on behalf of someone or something brings me into another reality, beyond the dualities of good and bad, hope or despair. In a hotel room, in my friend Rose's hospital room, in my son Ken's dying room, as I move slowly and gracefully, the movements smooth out the rough places inside my body and change the energy in the room. It takes me to the place the eleventh-century nun and composer Hildegard of Bingen sang of, "All is well, all is well, all manner of things are well." In our day, we would call this the place of serenity.

Still, The Big Suck didn't let up, and telling ourselves, "We'll do X when Y happens" or looking forward to "when this is all over" quit working too. Most days we just became determined to live as fully as possible in the middle of it. Our twenty-fifth wedding anniversary occurred the spring after the transplant, and Pearl wanted to send us on a Mediterranean cruise as a gift. Given her worry about how her son was managing under such tremendous stress, she urged us to go on the cruise sooner rather than later. The idea seemed totally nutty to me. How would we enjoy ourselves? How could we even focus? But when I mentioned the cruise to Corinne, she thought it was a great idea.

"Don't let my cancer ruin your whole life," she said. "I'm trying to keep it from totally ruining mine."

Corinne's friends said, "Go on our behalf, since we can't go. Besides, it's only for a week."

So we went on the cruise and lit a candle for Corinne, for ourselves, and for her friends and members of our communities in every shrine, cathedral, and chapel we passed on the continent. A friend had given me a book about the Black Madonna, an ancient archetypical image that represents the feminine face of God. The book contained a map to where her statues and iconic pictures were located, and this guided our wanderings, creating a kind of pilgrimage, taking us beyond the usual places featured on tourist maps.

From Mother Nature, an aspect of Isis in Egypt, to Our Lady of

Guadalupe, the patron of Mexico, to the monastery we visited at Montserrat near Barcelona, the Black Madonna represents the birthing and nurturing of children, the creative force of new life in the dark earth, the transformation of seeds into plants that feed the world, and, most importantly for me at that time, the honoring of the sacred journey toward death and rebirth. Like the Greek goddess Demeter, who went into the underworld to rescue her daughter, and the Indian goddess Kali, who destroys life in order to re-create it in a new form, these female figures of god comforted my mother's broken heart.

Of course, during the week of the trip there was the occasional crisis, mostly connected to how my body was handling stress. A year before we knew about Corinne's cancer challenge, my stomach had become overreactive and hypersensitive to some foods. The condition had started after exposure to poison oak in my Texas backyard, which seemed to happen repeatedly each summer. I would take the prescribed medicine, which was then decreased slowly till it wasn't needed anymore. But after one particular annual episode, I couldn't get off the medicine. Every time I tried, my eyes swelled, my stomach burned, and my face sported a red rash. And it wasn't easy to figure out what foods were triggering it. It happened so frequently on Wednesday evenings that the members of my women's group teased that I must be allergic to *them*. Finally, one specialist suggested I avoid any food whose molecular structure was similar to poison oak, such as watermelon and most peppers. This solved part of the mystery, since our staff's Wednesday lunch meetings were held at a Mexican restaurant.

By the time of the cruise, I had learned to live with my food issues, after a fashion. I brought a list of foods to avoid, an anaphylactic kit, and a note from my doctor to assist medical personnel in case I needed treatment. The evening before docking in Italy, we were served a mild and delicious curry soup. In retrospect, it seems the only possible offender, and as a result I missed Rome. Rich toured by himself, and I spent a day and night in my stateroom doubled over in pain. Once it was out of my system, I was okay, but from that experience we developed a new standard for cuisine: Does it taste good enough to miss Rome for?

"I don't want you to come to Houston this next time, Mom. I want to go by myself," Corinne told me in a phone conversation. I got that arrow-piercing, deeply hurt feeling in the pit of my stomach, like I'd gotten when she called twelve years before to tell me that I had a grandson. That good news had come with a sharp jab to my middle since I had had a suitcase packed for over a week, waiting for her call to let me know she was in labor. So what if I was in Texas? The plan had been for me to leave for Nebraska as soon as she called. Since the average labor for a first baby is sixteen hours, it didn't seem impossible that I could get there in time for some part of the birthing process. But she and Bill had decided to wait until the baby came to call me. After the initial shock, I knew I had to get over my hurt and get on with being a grandmother.

"I've been fired from my caregiver job," I told my friend Carol in our weekly phone conversation. "After two years as Corinne's caregiver, she said she didn't want me to go with her on her next visit to the cancer center. I didn't tell her how much that hurt my feelings."

"You can't fire your mother," Carol said in a definitive, offhanded tone. "It's impossible."

"I know she suspects the news is not going to be good. She wants to go by herself, no friends or family. I think she doesn't want to have to take care of anyone else when she gets more bad news."

With Carol's encouragement, I called my daughter and made my case for her to allow me to join her. "I'm not going for *you,* Corinne. I'm going for *me.* You know how hard it is to understand what the doctors are saying. Even when I'm in the room with them, it's hard to grasp their meaning. I just can't imagine trying to get everything secondhand. You don't have to take care of me, Corinne. I just know that being there is a better way for me to take care of myself."

"Oh," she said with a tone of surprise in her voice. "I wish Bill would do that."

When she mentioned Bill, my heart went out to him. Her comment reminded me of an earlier conversation they'd had, which she shared with me.

"Bill said he feels bad that he can't cheer me up. He says, 'Your friends, other people can cheer you up, but I can't.'" Corinne had told him, "I think, well, let's see, I look at you and I see the man I love, that I have been married to for nearly twenty years, and whom I may be leaving to raise our three children alone. Yes, you're right. When I look at you, it doesn't cheer me up."

Corinne finally agreed to have both Bill and me accompany her to Houston. We went and had a surprisingly wonderful time, in the midst of what was not good news. We ate at a Japanese restaurant recommended by her Japanese transplant doctor and at a Mexican restaurant recommended by the infusion therapist. (No peppers for me!) We visited people who by now had become dear friends: the fiftyish gay man who staffed the volunteer center on Wednesdays and who had dried Corinne's tears on previous bad-news days. This time, Corinne comforted him: *his* cancer had come out of remission.

On this, what turned out to be our final visit to the center, I couldn't resist checking each woman's restroom we passed. I found, with great relief, that the obnoxious "You Can Prevent Cancer" signs had been removed—*all but one.* I knew it was an oversight. The maintenance crew had removed the bolts that held the sign in the plastic holder, but the last lonely sign was still in place. With just a small effort of my fingernail, I removed the remaining copy of the sign and waved it triumphantly over my head as I ran into the hallway to show my daughter my accomplishment.

Though I wasn't sure why I did it at the time, I brought the sign home as a souvenir. It seemed a symbol of how a small mistake can have a big, ongoing negative effect. Looking back now, I can feel almost grateful to the sign for giving me a concrete place to focus my anger and sense of helplessness as I accompanied my daughter on her medical treatment journey. A journey where the effects of early mistakes made by well-meaning professionals could not be undone and in the end almost certainly prevented a positive outcome. Though pitifully inadequate compared to the enormity of all that needs to change in our health care system, I take some comfort in that one small instance where being persistent enough made positive change possible.

SAYING GOOD-BYE

It was the middle of August 2004 and fortunately not as hot as it could be in Nebraska at that time of year. But there was the usual summer sticky feeling on my skin, the slight dampness at the roots of my hair provoked by the slightest physical activity. The activity in my daughter's gray-and-white frame house revolved around a hospital bed in the small den off the kitchen. Friends, family members, and various health care professionals came and went, tending to Corinne, who was now gravely ill.

The prior evening when I came into the kitchen from the den, I found Bill pacing back and forth across the room. He was clutching a tea towel, wiping counters with one hand and picking up the kids' school papers with the other. His eyes narrowed as he turned around, stopped moving, and looked directly at me.

"If she doesn't show some signs of getting better by tomorrow, she's going to the hospital. We can't take care of her here."

"I agree with you, Bill, but she doesn't want to go."

"She's not thinking clearly. The cancer has affected her brain. I've been through this before. Corinne and I saw the same thing with my mother and her breast cancer. Towards the end, the cancer affected her brain."

I didn't argue with him. But I felt that, although she might go in and out of her rational mind, it was important for her to still make decisions about her own life.

Before it became a sick room, the den served as a communication and organizing center for the household. A wooden computer cabinet with a printer and a corkboard posted with sheets of phone numbers and the kids' sports teams' schedules kept the family on top of who needed to be where and when. Across from the computer cabinet, Corinne's grandfather's antique desk was the spot for sorting mail, paying bills, and shredding advertising flyers. A beige suede love seat, nestled in a front alcove of the room, was just the right size for reading or being read to from one of the many books on the floor-to-ceiling bookcase wall.

The current scene was not something that had ever been imagined for this space by the family or anyone who knew them. Corinne and Bill had met in high school as cheerleader and football player, courted long distance during college, and married a year or so after graduation. He earned an MBA, she a physical therapy degree, before they started their family. Independent, capable, and responsible, they were most often the ones who helped others. But now those tables had turned.

Throughout the past two and a half years, Bill and Corinne's friends from high school, co-workers from the physical therapy clinic, neighbors, parents of the children's friends, and ladies from their small church all took turns tending to the needs of this family. It was difficult at first, especially for Bill, to accept so much help from people. But Corinne told him, "People want to help. They want to *do something.* You know how good it feels for us to give to someone else. Well, that's what we are giving to them when we *let* them help."

For two and a half years, someone delivered a meal to this house five evenings a week. Someone shopped for birthday presents and Christmas gifts, and someone wrapped them. Someone drove the kids to soccer and basketball practice, piano lessons, and play dates when Mom and Dad were out of town for her treatments. Someone handled her e-mail communication to keep everyone informed of her progress and what tasks needed doing. The only glitch involved some ladies from church who didn't have e-mail. They complained that all the dates to bring meals were often taken before they had a chance to sign up!

This self-organized village did whatever it could, all the while hoping and praying it would be enough. Enough to avoid what was happening now.

This morning, the home health nurse had called us into the living room. Speaking softly so Corinne could not hear, the nurse explained that the swelling in her ankles and the puffiness in her arms and legs were signs her kidneys were failing.

"How could this be happening?" I thought to myself in horror. I recalled how, when I was in the hospital with Rose, a nurse explained that for death to occur, *a major organ system has to fail*. And when my son Ken was close to death, the doctor who came by the house told us it's especially hard to predict the time of death for young people, because *a major organ system has to fail,* and their organs are young and healthy in spite of their illness.

Now this nurse is telling us that Corinne's kidneys are failing. That means she is dying. But I told myself, "I've seen this before, her seemingly being close to death." In the previous two and a half years, during some of her procedures, she seemed close to death—like several months after the transplant, when her fever went to 105 degrees while a blotchy red rash covered her entire body. After a tenuous night in the ER, her doctors brought the GVH under control, and her system returned to balance.

Anytime things weren't looking good, Corinne would remind me of her friend Sherry, an exceptional patient we'd met at M.D. Anderson. "Sherry was close to death many times," Corinne would say. Unsaid was the fact we both clung to: after all her medical emergencies, Sherry *survived* and was healthy today.

>>> ■ <<<

The computer cabinet across from the bed was finally closed. The night before, with my assistance, Corinne had struggled into a wheelchair and then to the computer keyboard to complete her final written response to a newspaperwoman who'd been following her breast cancer journey. The last installment of the three-part story on Corinne was to run in the newspaper that day, and the reporter wanted to include Corinne's response in her own words.

"She has more important things on her mind right now than that, Sheila," Bill barked at me from the other room when he overheard me mentioning the reporter's phone call.

I thought, "I'm not sure there is anything more important. This may be one of the last things she needs and wants to do."

Anger had become Bill's knee-jerk reaction lately as his wife continued to slip away from him and the area of his responsibilities mounted. In the last few weeks I had become a prime target of his anger. After the home health nurse's pronouncements that Corinne was dying, Bill's impatience with me increased. He refused to use the notebook that friends and family caregivers were using to keep track of the timing and doses of Corinne's medications. In reading through it, I asked him if and when he had given her morphine. "Just never mind, Sheila, I have everything under control," he said in a gruff voice that trailed behind me as I walked out of the room.

I left the room so as not to fight back or break down in front of my daughter and her friends and the nurse. "Okay Bill," I stormed to myself. "If that's true, then fix this situation, for Corinne and for all of us."

"We don't need any upset here, and we don't need any out there either," Bill yelled after me.

The nurse followed me into the living room and began to explain the situation as she saw it. "He's just upset. You will need to be the bigger person," she said. "Do you have family or friends here? Maybe you could take a break and be with them for a while." In that moment, I realized the extent of my isolation and aloneness.

"No, that is my daughter lying in there. I live in Texas. I don't have friends or other family members here."

"Well then, why don't you take a little walk?"

What else was there to do? I left the house through the front door, taking only my cell phone. I began walking, swiftly at first, through the well-manicured neighborhood. My effort seemed to have a paradoxical effect, however. Instead of expending my pent-up energy, each step on the pavement seemed to dare my emotions to erupt, breaking whatever composure I had been able to accomplish throughout these recent agonizing days. As I walked I began making phone calls, reaching out for a voice of someone I knew, someone who cared about me. And with each attempt, my sense of isolation grew. My husband's phone went directly to voice mail. Glenda's line gave a continuous ring that meant her answering machine was full or she was on the computer.

Around the corner from the house, the sidewalk narrowed, carrying me through an overgrown wooded area, a shortcut for people on their way to a large contemporary church structure, the cathedral for the Catholic diocese. I crossed the boulevard, walked into the church garden, and then into the building itself. Sunlight streamed through the stained-glass windows, lighting the vestibule. Otherwise, the church was dark except for the small flickering of votive candles.

It was early afternoon, and only a couple of people were in the church. I walked around inside the cavernous structure, clutching my cell phone, hoping it would ring yet wondering what I would do if it did. Smelling the candles and seeing the altars decorated with flowers and statues of various saints reminded me of other churches and other occasions. My Irish Catholic mother and five-year-old me, lighting candles for my infant baby sister, my elementary school years, attending daily Mass and singing in the choir for weekend weddings and funerals. Our trip to Europe the previous spring, when Rich and I lit a candle for Corinne in every church we came across. But I found no comfort now in what seemed a gigantic mausoleum.

Standing under a tree on the church grounds, I finally reached my friend Carol. I immediately launched into a lament about the difficulties between Bill and me. "Do I have to leave my daughter's deathbed in order for her to die in peace?" I sobbed into the phone.

"You are not alone," she said. "Just stay in the corner of the room at the foot of her bed and meditate. I'll be with you, praying for you and Corinne and Bill. Tell me what the room looks like." Realizing she would be sharing this vigil with me from afar calmed my insides and dried my tears.

Before going back to the house, I got my husband on his cell phone. "You must come NOW," I demanded. He said he had a ticket to come in a couple of days. My voice grew louder and more insistent. "I need you here NOW." Only after he agreed to try to get a flight out that night or the next morning did I end the conversation and walk back toward the house.

Approaching Bill and Corinne's house, I remembered how, after a long exhaustive search, they had found it six years before. Bill's parents discovered the For Sale sign during one of their exercise walks, when Wilma was nearing the end of her life, and she died before they moved in.

Coming into the driveway, I noticed the basketball hoop that Corinne had bought recently to replace the old one. Three-year-old Will had known this was the right house because it came with a basketball hoop in the driveway. Coming from a two-bedroom, one-bath cottage, five-year-old Ethan had run up and down the stairs in this three-story house, squealing with delight as he counted the bathrooms. When they moved in, Tori was not quite a year old, but she came to love having her own room, decorated by her mom with handmade yellow-and-pink window valances and matching pillows and bedspread. Across the top of the front wall, Corinne had stenciled: "Vitoria Victorious, Delight thyself also in the Lord; and He shall give thee the desires of thine heart. Psalm 37:4."

Standing at the foot of Corinne's bed as Carol had instructed me to do, my mind recounted all the work Corinne and Bill had done to make the house just right for their family. How many evenings and weekends it took for several years—replacing carpeting with hardwood floors, exchanging paint and fabric swatches to get just the right match, even negotiating ladders to hand-paint vertical stripes on the walls of the two-story entry hall. George, during his twice-a-year visits from Oregon, added crown molding in the living room and installed a traditional-style mantel over the 1960s fireplace. During visits to North Texas, Corinne and I took advantage of that shopper's wonderland to find the unique touches: drawer pulls, curtain fabric, lamps, and picture frames. All done with the infinite loving effort it took to make this house a home.

>>> ▥ <<<

Bill went upstairs to talk with the children; I assumed he was preparing them to say good-bye to their mother. While he was gone, Corinne said, "I don't want him to talk to them." I asked what she did want, and she said, "I want us to talk to them together . . . but not now." She sighed, "Things are moving so fast." All I could do was agree that they were.

After a few minutes the three children came downstairs and into the den. Ten-year-old William was hanging back behind his father. "I hate this," he said in a grumpy voice. Bill put his arm on Will's shoulder and guided him closer to his mother.

Corinne shifted into her protective mother role. "Nothing's changed. I'm not dying right now . . . I'm still taking the chemo. Just because my eyes are closed, it doesn't mean I'm dead. If you come home from school and you get concerned . . . " She paused. "Of course there will be someone with me . . . but if you are alone and get concerned, you can call 911."

Ethan got the idea of reading to his mother out of her Bible. He picked a passage that she had marked as one of her favorites, 2 Corinthians, 12.9: "My grace is sufficient for thee, for strength is made perfect in weakness. Gladly therefore I will glory in my infirmities, that the strength of Christ may dwell in me. . . . For when I am weak, then I am strong."

Tori, who had celebrated her seventh birthday only two days before with a swimming party, curled up beside her mom and laid her head on her mother's shoulder. Will draped himself over the foot of the bed and then later, as they were about to leave, he moved to the love seat, not wanting to leave the room.

Ethan began to cry, and Corinne spoke directly to him, "I'm not dying now. Of course, I've never died before, but we know someone who has—the person on our favorite TV show." The kids looked at each other, not sure what she was referring to, but Ethan quickly figured out it was the show *Touched by an Angel*. The story's main character has come back to life after dying to help people still living on earth.

Corinne repeated again, "I'm not dying *now*, but we don't know when it will be— could be tomorrow, could be the next day—it all depends on what number is written down in God's book. (This related to the Bible passage she had read to the children about how each person is given a certain number of days of life.)

"Remember," she said in a simple teaching voice, "it isn't what we want. It's what God wants."

She talked especially to Will, telling him how much she loved him and reassuring him that God was looking out for him.

The kids hugged their mother and went off to go swimming with their aunt and cousins. Corinne drifted off to sleep. During this whole session, I felt extremely uncomfortable. We all knew Corinne's status— that she was dying—but she did not. Remembering the horrific sound Ken had made when Kevin told him he was dying, I didn't want to tell Corinne. I didn't want anyone to tell her. While standing at the foot of her bed, I prayed silently that she would come to know the truth of her situation herself. If it were true she was in fact dying, perhaps her guardian angel or Jesus himself could come to her and let her know.

A nurse came by the house to check on the breathing machine that Corinne used in the night, and she urged Bill to make a decision for hospice, either in the home or at the hospital. Bill decided he needed to take Corinne back to the hospital, and he attempted to talk with her about it. He told Corinne that they could keep her more comfortable at the hospital than we could at home.

Corinne twisted up out of her bed, abruptly. "DAMN it, Bill, I'm DYING. LEAVE ME ALONE!" She collapsed back onto the bed, her back turned to him.

Corinne's outburst and the shock that Bill and I were experiencing seemed to suck the air out of the room. Later Bill told me he'd *never* heard his wife curse in all their twenty-five years together. As much as I wanted my daughter to remain undisturbed in her own home, and as much as the thought of getting her to the hospital seemed an almost insurmountable task, I moved from the foot of the bed to her side and began supporting Bill's effort.

"Well, Corinne, if what you said is true, then Bill's just trying to get you to keep your agreement. Remember, you said you did not want to die in this house. You said, 'This can be the house where mommy was sick, but the house could never be the same for the children if this is the house where mommy died.'"

She gave a sigh and agreed to go to the hospital. I went upstairs to rest. I was reeling from the dramatic change in Corinne's attitude, the fact that she did comprehend her situation, and that it seemed to occur in response to my prayer. In about a half hour, one of Corinne's friends came upstairs bringing a message from Bill: "Do you want to travel in the ambulance with Corinne to the hospital? Bill will drive behind in his car."

"Yes," I said, grateful he was granting me this privilege.

Once Corinne was settled into her room, Bill decided to go and get the children from his brother's wife. "We can't just sneak their mother out of the house when they aren't there and have her die without them being able to say good-bye," Bill said.

I looked at him in amazement, as I had many times in the past two and a half years since Corinne's diagnosis. How tuned-in this professional banker was, continuously and accurately, to his children's needs. Of course the children needed to be able to say good-bye. I, the social worker grandmother, agreed. I'd been so focused on my daughter that I'd lost track of the children.

>>> ▪ <<<

The three kids entered the hospital/hospice room a short time later, accompanied by their father and Grandpa Don. They entered tentatively, respectfully, their footsteps barely making a sound on the tile floor. Corinne sat propped up in bed and smiled gently as each of her children approached and gave her a hug. She tried to speak but had trouble forming the words.

"Just a minute . . . " she said clearly, and then there was a long pause. "Just . . . a . . . minute . . . " she said again slowly in a strong voice, followed by another long pause. She closed her eyes and struggled to access her words.

The children reached out to her. "Take your time, Mommy. Take your time."

"Oh no, she's waited too long," I thought as a feeling of dread overtook me. I recalled Ken and Rose no longer being able to form words near the end.

Seeing her mother struggling to speak, Tori left the comfort of her father's arms. Leaning over the bedside and placing her small seven-year-old hand on top of her mother's, she said in her most grown-up, comforting voice, "It's okay, Mommy. Take your time."

Both boys were openly crying now, and Tori moved closer to her dad, crawling inside his arms as a sea creature might crawl into its protective shell. I stood next to Ethan on the opposite side of the bed, continually handing him tissues to wipe his tears.

Holding his glasses in my hand and feeling the scratchy texture of the cheap tissues, I had the strangest thought: "Either the hospital is saving lots of money or their supplier is getting rich on this item." As the tissue exchange continued, I began saying to Ethan and Will, "Here, have another piece of *sandpaper*," which seemed an accurate description.

Bill told us he wanted to talk to Corinne alone, so Bill's dad and I took the children down a long corridor to the family reception room. We had barely arrived at the room when we were called back. Again Corinne tried to talk but couldn't form the words. As the boys continued crying, I thought, "How will we ever move from this place to the next place? How will we ever finish this and be able to leave here?"

Finally I began talking. Like a translator, I repeated everything I'd ever heard Corinne say about her children and about leaving them.

"What you are trying to say is that you are not worried about your children, right?" I said looking directly at her.

Corinne nodded her head, affirming what I was saying.

"You know that they have the best dad in the world."

She nodded.

"You love these children very much. You don't want to leave them, but it is not what you want but what God wants."

Corinne's face showed tremendous relief as she shook her head in the affirmative.

"You're not worried about your children because you know that God loves them, and they will do well because you have given them to God."

Now it seemed Corinne was affirming my words with her whole body.

"And now, *we* must give *you* to God."

Yes, her head nodded slowly.

"You also know that you can continue to be their mother—to watch over them from wherever you are and wherever they are."

Ethan responded enthusiastically to this notion. "Mommy, you will be with me every time I read my Bible." Looking around the room, he said, "Oh, we should have brought her Bible."

On that cue, Bill reached his right hand into the drawer of the bedside table beside him and produced a Bible. This Bible, being supplied by the hospital, was not marked with her favorite passages. I wiped Ethan's glasses so he could read, and I asked if he knew a particular passage he would like to read. He shook his head no, opened the Bible at random, and began reading. The story he'd come upon was about Moses. It described the exact moment when Moses realized, because he was old and sick and couldn't stand up, that he would *not* be able to take his people into the Promised Land. Someone else would have to do it: "I am now 120 years old and am no longer able to lead you; The Lord has said to me 'You shall not cross the Jordan.' The Lord your God himself will cross over ahead of you."

I was blown away by the appropriateness of the passage. When Ethan finished, he said with excitement in his voice, "Did you like that, Mommy?"

Corinne smiled proudly, letting him know that she did.

Someone said it was time to go. One at a time, each child hugged their mother, and I hugged each of them as they left the room.

Corinne fell back onto the bed and into a deep sleep. A nurse who came in a few minutes later to check her stats told me later that she had no idea how Corinne was able to focus and be present with her children given her numbers on the monitoring equipment attached to her. In the midst of my overwhelming sorrow, I felt tremendous pride in my daughter and grandchildren and a sense of awe and gratitude for my part in this sacred drama.

MIDWIFERY AGAIN

It was hard to imagine how Corinne was hanging on. Her kidneys had begun failing Sunday morning, and here it was Wednesday. Sunday afternoon she'd said good-bye to her three children. Out-of-town relatives had begun arriving: Rich from Texas, Kevin from California, aunts Pat and Mary Jane from Detroit, cousin Tammy from Louisville. They'd each had some time with her, and though she didn't seem awake, she wasn't exactly asleep either. The only close family member missing was George, her biological father.

George's sister Beth called from Chicago: "George told me he isn't coming until the funeral. I'm not sure that's a good idea. He might regret it afterwards. Should I make him come?"

"My concern is for Corinne. I don't want her waiting for him if he isn't coming. But no, I don't think you should make him come. George has a heart condition, and he knows at some level what he can handle."

I told Corinne, "Your father loves you very much, and he will be here afterwards for the children. You need to take care of yourself now. You don't have to wait for him or for anyone."

Early afternoon, partly as an excuse to get out in the fresh air and partly to avoid hospital food, Rich and I walked across the street to get something to bring back to eat. Our only option was a barbecue restaurant, and as we entered, I felt transported to Texas in the late 1800s, but for the flat-screen TV and the blinking neon beer signs. As we stood waiting at the takeout counter, a pain began to throb in the center of my abdomen. I felt like I was carrying the weight of the entire world in my belly. It was a physical pain, but as I stayed with it, I recognized it as sorrow, what my friend Glenda calls women's work—"bearing the unbearable." My mind was full of questions: What could be keeping her here? Is there something I need to do to help her cross? Am I holding on to her in some way that I'm not aware of? Does she need something from me? Clearer permission to go? Instruction on how to let go?

I remembered something I'd heard in Brazil, through one of my traveling mates, "Your daughter is afraid she will break your heart." The intensity of my pain increased, and I realized the pain wasn't just mine. It was the sorrow of all the people who loved Corinne and who didn't want her to go. Perhaps it was even her own sorrow—the sorrow of a mother who fears she is breaking *her* children's hearts.

By now the pain had become so intense that I was doubled up and could barely stand. I prayed to the Brazilian entities, especially my case manager: "Please help me to know what I must do and help me to do it." When we got back to the hospital, I retrieved Kevin from the family waiting room, where he was talking with relatives. I told him I wanted him to come with me as I talked with Corinne, as I said my good-bye to her.

In Corinne's room, Kevin and I began talking about Margaret, the woman who had taken care of Corinne and her brothers when they were small, growing up in Detroit. Margaret had called with a message for Corinne about how much she loved her and how sorry she was to not be able to be with us. In the thirty years since Margaret had been in the role of raising the children, we'd often called on her for her wisdom. I told Corinne what Margaret had said to me: "You know, Sheila, you have to give your children to God. And I know you do. But then, I know you—and you take them back."

"I told Margaret she was right, Corinne, and that I'm working on it."

Leaning over the side of the bed, close to Corinne's ear, I said, "You've done all the hard things, and now the hard part is finished. What you need to do now will be the *easiest* thing you've ever done in your life. There are people waiting for you on the other side: Ken and Rose, Wilma and Auntie. All those people who have crossed over and who love you so much. Papa Joe, Grandma Jane. Just take their hands, and they will take you home. They will take you to Jesus." I kissed her forehead and whispered, "I love you very much. You have done such a good job with your life and with your children. I'm so proud of you."

And then, although it wasn't anything I'd planned or thought about ahead of time, I turned to Kevin, who, as Corinne's younger brother, grew up letting her speak for him when they were small children. "Now it's time for you to find your voice with your sister." And I walked out of the room.

>>> ■ <<<

Standing in the hallway outside her room were some of Corinne's girlfriends, and one of them asked me about my trip to Brazil. While we were talking, I became aware of my body and noticed that the pain was completely gone. I felt an ethereal lightness of being. In a few minutes, Bill had someone call me back into the room. As I entered, I saw Bill leaning over the top of Corinne's bed with his arms around her and Kevin still seated at her other side.

"There's not much left," Bill said, and I felt her energy waning. I saw an image of streaming strings of light breaking their bonds with her body as her spirit was leaving. I thought, "If those strings were connected to all the people who wanted her to stay, no wonder it took her so long to leave." Thoughts raced through my head: the notion of the bodhisattva, a person who stays a bit longer on this plane to heal others instead of going directly on to a new life. I thought of Corinne's faith in Jesus's sacrifice. I thought of what she herself had written just a few nights before, in her response to the newspaper story about her journey with breast cancer:

> Reading my story is far from encouraging if you just hear
> the story over and over. . . . This is a story about growing
> in faith, depending on God's provision. . . . I have tried to

do the right and Godly ways but it is not our acts that bring us to kneel before him. Instead of Him being a part of this world and His attention revolving around me, I AM HERE TO SERVE Him, and I revolve around HIM.

I can say I would trade this cancer experience but am still working on realizing [that] the meaning of this will come as I approach His throne and he calls me his good and faithful servant. . . . Rejoice in Him and look to Him for all you need.

As I looked down at Corinne's now lifeless body, I said to her indomitable spirit, "Well done, dearest Corinne. You have been a most good and faithful servant."

When the attendants came for her body, I thought, "Take it. Take her body. It's broken and it couldn't be fixed. She doesn't need it anymore." I walked beside the gurney as it bore her body down the darkened corridor. A lone man was standing silently at attention in the distance. I recognized him as one of Corinne's doctors, the one who'd tried to discourage us from getting a third opinion in Houston.

At the time, Rich and I were furious with him for what seemed to us his attempt to take Corinne's hope away. But that anger was gone now, at least from my body. As we passed him, I saw from his slumped shoulders and downcast eyes that he wasn't taking any glory from this turn of events that had proved him right.

That evening, I spoke with Kevin. "You don't have to tell me if you don't want to, but I am more than a little curious about what you said to your sister."

He began with a wary smile. "I told her, 'I know what I'm *supposed* to say, but I don't want you to go.' And then, after a few minutes I said, 'I don't have any words of wisdom. The only thing I do know is love is easy and love never dies.'"

"That sounds pretty wise to me," I told him. And then we hugged.

ASHES

What about the ashes?" George asked Bill, who was seated at the computer desk, typing out something he wanted to be read at Corinne's memorial service.

"I don't know."

"I was thinking," George continued. "What about taking them to Michigan to inter them where Ken's are? My sister Mary can make arrangements for that."

Standing nearby, I had an immediate negative reaction, but I tried to be rational in making my case. "I don't think that's a good idea, George. Corinne's family is here, and Michigan is too far away from the kids. They have no way to get up there to visit."

Bill looked up from the screen at me and said abruptly, "Take them. Do whatever you want with them."

His words knocked the breath out of me. I felt like I'd been slugged in the stomach. Seconds later, trying to recover, I began questioning myself as to why I was having such a strong reaction. I was shocked at Bill's seeming indifference to what would happen to Corinne's ashes, but there was something else I didn't have words to explain, even to myself. Finally, I realized I felt a terrible, overwhelming responsibility.

I'd known that Corinne was going to be cremated. She must have mentioned it, but we never talked about what she wanted done with her ashes. Nine years before, at Rose's request, Rich and I had gone with Rose's daughter to take her ashes to the beach at Corpus Christi.

We had a lovely ceremony, telling our personal stories of Rose, and then we opened the bag that contained the ashes, scooped them into our hands, and held them into the wind. A gentle breeze carried them out to sea.

Corinne knew about the beachside ceremony we had for Rose, but she never said anything about it one way or the other. She never commented on the cemetery where we took her brother's ashes. And Bill's mother Wilma—I remember her funeral and burial in the family plot in Lincoln. I guess I had assumed that Bill would bury his wife with *his* family members.

As I began walking out of the room, I heard Bill's voice say again, "Take 'em and do what you want with them. But, I'll tell you this, she wasn't big about taking up space."

"I guess that means no burial," I thought to myself.

Later, I remembered the twins. Bill and Corinne had buried their unborn twins in a Catholic cemetery in Lincoln. Though not Catholic, they shared the Catholic Church's belief that life begins at conception. I never questioned it. I assumed they wanted to make it clear that their unborn children were human lives. I remembered how their little boys, five and three at the time, never failed to mention the twins whenever we drove past the cemetery. "There's where the twins are," they would tell me. "Hi twins!" they would call out, waving through the window of the car. And this practice went on for several years. The twins stayed part of the family simply because they were buried in a place we often drove by.

As I grappled with what would be the right thing to do with Corinne's ashes, I thought of a cousin's story about growing up having picnics on summer holidays in the field where our ancestors are buried in rural Illinois. She said the kids were especially intrigued by one particular gravestone of a baby that had died at a month old. Had he lived, that baby would have been their uncle, so upon arriving at the site, they always raced to find the gravestone, saying, "Hi, Uncle Arnie."

Since I didn't know what to do with the ashes, I had to take them home with me to Texas until I decided. I cringed at the idea of bringing them with me on the plane. Although the funeral home would provide a certificate identifying the box as a person's remains, it gave me the creeps imagining Homeland Security people rifling through and finding Corinne's ashes. "Maybe I'm making too big a deal of the ashes," I chided myself. The ashes were not my daughter, I knew that, but still, my Catholic upbringing taught me that ashes are sacred and the bones of saints holy, even capable of bringing forth miracles. Perhaps that was the root of my reverence for Corinne's physical remains, the part of her that had come from my physical body.

Kevin agreed to drive Corinne's ashes in his car (along with his suitcases and two dogs) and drop them off to me in Texas on his way home to California. Once they arrived safely, I placed the unadorned box on the altar in my bedroom underneath a statue of a guardian angel, gifted to me by former clients when Ken had died.

>>> ■ <<<

"Grief takes your chi," my acupuncturist said when I told him how fatigued I'd been since returning from my daughter's funeral. "I'm having trouble eating, not because I'm not hungry but mostly because I don't have the energy to hold my fork."

There was a lot to be tired from. There'd been two funerals in Lincoln for Corinne, the first on Friday night at Bill's family's small Germans-from-Russia ancestral church. This service was attended mostly by *our* family and close friends. Bill had known that Corinne's side of the family would want to celebrate her life by telling stories, singing, and dancing as we'd done at Ken's service. So he arranged for his church to host this celebration, which, except for the lack of alcohol, was probably reminiscent of what our Irish or Scottish ancestors might have done. After the service, Tori suggested we go to TCBY, one of her mother's favorite spots, and Grandpa George supported her idea. I can still see Tori and three of her seven-year-old girlfriends, their heads huddled together at the small children's table, giggling over their yogurt, losing themselves in one another's company.

The second, more formal service needed to be held in a much larger church, especially since the three-part series about Corinne's journey with breast cancer had just run in the local paper. We were advised to expect *a thousand people,* and that's pretty close to how it turned out. Bill's older brother coordinated this service. His job became running back and forth between Bill, who was stationed at the computer in the den, and family and friends seated at the picnic table in the backyard.

We were told that this service was to be for "the people-of-faith," which I took to mean that Corinne's Jewish stepfather and her spiritually eclectic mother were to stay out of it. As much as I wanted Bill to have whatever he wanted in this service, memories of my father-in-law's funeral were still fresh in my mind. Five years prior, when Rich's father had died, his mother made Rich promise not to mention his stepchildren in the eulogy he delivered. With Corinne and my father and sister in the audience, the ceremony had felt especially dishonoring to my family. I shared my worry with Rich that Corinne's service might feel similarly excluding of us. So when Rich heard there was to be a reading from the Old Testament, he volunteered to be that reader. "That fellow's from my tribe," he said of the passage's writer, thereby turning his difference into an asset. His proposal went back and forth between Bill and the people at the picnic table until it got an okay. And though I find no mention of this in the program, my recollection is that Rich and I read together a passage from the Old Testament selected by Bill and the people-of-faith committee.

A central element of the service was a slide show of pictures of Corinne played on a large screen behind the altar. But as the proud grandmother, one of the most outstanding features for me was twelve-year-old Ethan playing the piano. Bill had been quite protective of Ethan, not wanting him to be pressured into doing something he didn't feel ready to do. But Ethan insisted he wanted to play, and he beamed when people told him how proud they were of him.

"And you know who else is really proud of you today?" I asked.

He answered with a shy smile and downcast eyes, "My mother."

Someone organized a buffet luncheon at the large church, which was wonderful because we had so many out-of-town guests. There were Corinne's Chi Omega sorority friends from around the country, who'd taken turns to be with her in Houston and Lincoln. Glenda, Carol, and several other women from my women's spirituality group either drove the eleven hours from Texas or flew through Chicago to get to Nebraska. My siblings who had been at Ken's service were there, as well as my sister's daughter, placed for adoption when she was born. Lynn had recently found her biological mother, and we were able to meet the mother who raised her, making it a real gathering of the clan.

Hosting and housing for all these out-of-towners was made possible through the generosity of the mother of one of Corinne's friends. Since she had recently moved in with her daughter's family, she had a large, fully furnished house standing vacant only a few blocks from Corinne and Bill's. This became our home base as people arrived from everywhere at all hours of the day and night. It reminded me of Corinne's wedding, which was held in Lincoln, though I had hoped to have it in Texas. Corinne made the decision for Lincoln, but she quieted my objections by renting an entire historical bed-and-breakfast mansion for our family's out-of-town guests.

A few days after Corinne's funeral, I had the honor of getting Tori ready for her first day of school. The teacher had sent a note home telling her second-grade class what to bring, and one of the items was a hat. The note mentioned that each child would be asked to tell a story about the hat. Tori and I searched through the family closets, collecting a dozen or so hats, but she had trouble deciding which one to take. I suggested she sleep on the decision, so she put three on her dresser before climbing into bed. The following morning she bounded out of bed, knowing exactly which one to take. As she ran out the door, she grabbed the black baseball cap her mother had worn most every day of late to cover her hairless head. Clutching the hat in her small hands she told me, over her shoulder, "I know the most about this one."

Six weeks after the funeral, there was a memorial service for Corinne in Houston, organized by folks she'd met traveling back and forth for her treatments. Bill didn't want the kids involved since they were back in school and had already attended two services. He didn't want their structure and routine interrupted, and that sounded right to me.

So Rich, Kevin, and I represented the family at the Houston service. Kevin flew from LA to Dallas, and he and I drove together to Houston. Due to his work schedule, Rich needed to fly later from Fort Worth. When we picked him up at the Houston Airport, he seemed in a particularly bad mood. At the memorial, when it was his turn to read Bill's message, which was to be his part in the proceedings, he put his head down and shook it, as though he didn't have the energy to go on with it. Kevin stepped in, took the paper from him, and read it. An InterPlay friend played the flute as she had done at the women's prison when I taught there, and several other friends joined me in dancing on behalf of Corinne's passionate concerns. These concerns, such as improving the school lunch program and promoting exercise for children and elders to prevent obesity, were issues we would have to carry on without her, on her behalf.

I was surprised to see Corinne's bone marrow doctor there. He told me it was the first service he had ever attended for one of his patients. Tears came to my eyes when he said, "She was a very special person. It wasn't just how she handled her disease. It was how she handled her *life*."

Immanuel, the cab driver, arrived just after the service ended. He was flustered and apologetic as he told me he'd gotten lost. I found it hard to believe that a cab driver wouldn't have been able to find the First Christian Church, prominently located near the medical center. I took this to be a measure of how upset he was about Corinne's death.

After the service, Rich, Kevin, and I drove to Earthsprings, Glenda's retreat center in East Texas, where I had attended women's retreats for over a dozen years. My intention was to have a small ceremony with some of Corinne's ashes, placing them in the spots marking the four directions around the Medicine Lodge, where six years earlier I had placed some of Ken's. A men's retreat had just ended when we arrived. Some of the men there had supported Ken when he was diagnosed and had supported our family through our nearly ten years of trials and tragedies.

As we were preparing to take the ashes to the lodge, Rich became "unglued," as the expression goes. He refused to participate in the ceremony and did so by attacking me verbally. Glenda tried to mediate our conversation and interrupt his litany of my faults, but that was mostly a lost cause. Finally it was agreed that Rich would go for a walk with one of the men, and several other men would take Rich's place in supporting me and Kevin as we placed Corinne's ashes where I had placed her brother's.

It was a good resolution. Rich and I were unable to support one another, and we needed our extended community to stand with us, separately and together. Much later, when Rich finally told me what had happened as he flew into Houston, I got some understanding of what he was experiencing.

"Just one glimpse of the Houston skyline, and I felt like my guts were spilling out of my body. It brought back all the trips we'd made to support Corinne through her treatments—treatments that were all for nothing!"

>>> ■ <<<

Nine months later, Rich and I brought Corinne's ashes with us in the car as we drove to Pennsylvania, relocating for Rich's new job. The ashes took their place on the altar in our new bedroom. I knew it wasn't their final resting place, but friends had advised me to keep them safe until Corinne's children would be old enough to make a decision about what *they* wanted to do with them.

One evening, about six months after our move, Rich railed at me in the angry voice he'd been using quite often since Corinne had died, "And I want those ashes out of our bedroom, NOW."

"Too bad," I replied calmly, "because they are staying right here."

I knew this was Rich's grief talking. It was the same tone and tenor of communication I got on occasion from Kevin when I visited him in California and from my son-in-law when I visited him and the grandchildren in Nebraska. Wearing my social-work hat, I told myself, "Men grieve differently from women," but the wounding I felt from this "friendly fire" was nearly my undoing. Unlike the time I spent with Corinne, which, while painful, felt blessed and holy, having the men in my life stuck in the anger phase of grief and dumping it on me increased my sense of isolation and loss a hundredfold.

A year and a half after Corinne's death, I finally confronted Rich. In spite of fun, relaxation, and the company of friends at a New Year's InterPlay weekend, Rich had fired on me for an insignificant remark I'd made about the route home. Alone in our cabin at the retreat center, he took that occasion to list my faults and the flaws in my personality.

It took the rest of the weekend, with the support of friends, for me to recover from what seemed at the time a life-threatening injury to our relationship. We drove home, the way he wanted to go, amid a lot of silence. I mentioned calmly that I had a "noticing" for him and that whenever he felt ready to hear it, he should let me know. After breakfast the next day, Rich sat in a chair by the fireplace and, stiffening his body, with a tone of teasing in his voice, he said, "Okay, I'm ready. Let me have it."

I began simply. "Cynthia says that no one has to change, and I agree with that. I feel that way about everyone else in the world except *you*."

The look on his face let me know that I definitely had gotten his attention with that statement.

"Everyone else but me? Why's that?"

"I don't have any agreements with anyone else. But I do with you. And you aren't keeping your deal with me."

"What deal is that?"

"As part of our wedding ceremony, we vowed we'd each do our own emotional work so that our personal stuff wouldn't splash out on the other person and ruin our relationship. And you're not doing your work. You're not keeping your part of the deal."

So we went to a grief group for people who had lost someone close to them. When we came out, Rich noted with annoyance that I hadn't cried and he had. "Why was that?" he badgered me. We went to a marriage counselor, and Rich felt it made things worse to talk about it. I agreed that we weren't getting anywhere. It was possible that, as with the many parents reported on in the professional social work and psychology literature, the loss of a child would cost us our relationship as well. And though the professional literature isn't clear about why this happens so frequently, I began getting some strong clues.

I thought back to how our relationship had survived the first loss. What was different this time? There was the fact that it was the second time. Maybe there's a limit to how much loss a marriage relationship can survive. But there was another difference. Rich had wanted to establish a fund in Corinne's memory as part of a community foundation in the city where she lived. Our idea was to fund it and allow it to grow until the children were old enough to decide what projects they would like to fund in honor of their mother. We wanted Bill to join with us, but he didn't want to participate. He went with me to the foundation office to learn about the procedures, since I asked him to go. But he declined to join us, saying he was concerned he might disagree with Rich and me over where the funds should be expended and that that would be harmful to his relationship with us. "That's something I would never want to happen," he added.

On the suggestion of the officer from the foundation, Rich and I started the fund with the idea that Bill could join us later. But this put Corinne's friends in the middle between her parents and her husband.

Some friends had initiated a fund-raising project and expressed an interest in putting the money in her memorial fund, but they didn't want to hurt Bill's feelings. This whole situation was hurtful for all of us, but especially for Rich.

The Texas AIDS bike ride had been a big part of Rich's grief recovery after Ken died. He was able to honor Ken by training for and riding 500 miles across Texas, raising money and awareness about the disease. There seemed no such way to honor Corinne. There was the Susan G. Komen Race for the Cure that we'd done several times, with and without Corinne. One special time, then nine-year-old William's entire soccer team walked together for Team Corinne because, as the kids told a reporter, "Will is our friend."

But once Corinne was no longer a survivor of the disease, the happy faces of all those women survivors, the way they were honored and celebrated, had become a terrible reminder that for us the party was over. And though, as one sign on the race trail so truthfully stated, "Every woman is at risk for breast cancer," it's hard not to question why some are spared death and others are not. Hopefully, someday, through the money they're raising, research will figure that out.

THE GRANDMOTHER CEREMONY

"Today's the one-year anniversary of the day your mommy went to heaven," I told my three grandchildren as we gathered around the family's dinette table.

Eleven-year-old William's eyes widened. "Has it been that long *already*?"

"Yes, it's hard to believe, isn't it? But I have an idea of something special we can do to honor your mommy on her special day. We'll need some Magic Markers and crayons."

"I know where some are," Tori said, and she promptly leapt from her seat. She grabbed a chair, scooted it over to the desk in the kitchen, and stood on its seat. Climbing onto the countertop, she reached the upper cabinet and the family's school supplies stored there.

I took some uninflated Mylar balloons out of my shopping bag and placed them on the dinette table. "The idea here is to decorate these and write messages on them to your mother. Then later, we'll have them blown up, take them to a high hill in the park, and release them into the heavens."

I'd hardly finished the directions when all three children dove into the supplies like they were a plateful of cookies and they were *really* hungry. Thirteen-year-old Ethan began drawing x and o symbols for hugs and kisses around the outer edge of his circular balloon. Will and

Tori drew hearts and some flowers to go along with the central message, "We love you, Mommy. We miss you, Mommy."

I'd been in Nebraska for nearly a week, helping to celebrate Tori's eighth birthday and taking the kids on outings. I'd seen how bereft Bill seemed, lost in his own private world, except when engaged by the children. I wanted to talk with him about my ideas for this ceremony, to tell him why I thought such a thing was important. For thirty years, I'd heard clients in therapy describe a particular season or day of the year when they annually and inexplicably became depressed. They might tell me about driving carelessly, starting a fight with a boss or a spouse, or barely having the strength to get out of bed. On further exploratory questioning, I learned that these episodes often corresponded to an anniversary important to a deceased loved one—a birth or death day or the anniversary of an accident. Most importantly, the day was not marked or thought about consciously but remembered at some deeper level, emerging to cause trouble in their lives.

After Ken's death, I remembered these stories of my clients, and I decided to begin a practice of celebrating Ken, especially on his birthday and crossing day. On the first anniversary of his death, I happened to be meeting with an executive from Blue Cross and Blue Shield, exploring the possibility of reimbursements for a staying-healthy program I'd developed. As we drove to the meeting, I told the psychologist who was presenting with me, "Reforming the health care system, even in this tiny way, is a great way to celebrate my son. He would definitely approve." Most every year since, I've looked for projects and actions to take to honor him.

But I didn't say any of this to Bill. I watched and waited to see how *he* wanted to handle Corinne's anniversary, and it seemed he didn't want to mention it. Whenever I had the impulse to bring it up, something inside held me back. If I told him about the ceremony I was planning, he might forbid me to do it or, more likely, insist on coming along while not really wanting to be there. In either case, he would ruin it for the children and me. I finally decided this was a grandmother thing.

I would honor his way of grieving, and I would share with my grand-children something my wisdom told me would be good for them. In retrospect, this turned out to be a mistake, one that affected Bill's and my relationship negatively for the year that followed.

After decorating the balloons, the kids and I had met two of their mother's women friends for lunch at a small restaurant, and the plan was to see a movie afterward. The two younger children didn't like any of the offerings on the menu and sulked at the table. Typically, they weren't picky about food, so I took them across the street to a grocery store to see if they might find something there. As they dismissed the sandwiches in the deli case one after another, I knew it wasn't about the food. It was about how decorating the balloons had created a stronger realization of how much they missed their mother. The child therapist friend who had told me about the balloon ritual had not warned me about this possibility.

I chastised myself for not going ahead and releasing the balloons immediately rather than interrupting the process with lunch and a movie. But we had selected the early matinee because Will thought the later movie might make him late for football practice, which, in this sports-minded family, was a definite no-no. As it turned out, the *March of the Penguins* couldn't have been a better choice. The icy ter-rain on the screen was a welcome respite from the scorching August weather outside. The struggle of the adult penguins to breed and raise their young prompted my grandchildren to comment on how much trouble parents go through for their kids. The life cycle of birth and death, and the role of the community as a buffer from the harsh reali-ties of wind and weather, seemed especially relevant to what we had been through as a family in the last few years.

The next stop was the party store to get the balloons inflated. The kids chose to stay in the car in spite of my warning that it might get uncomfortably hot. We drove to Observation Hill, the highest point near the lake, and trudged through a freshly tilled cornfield, its stubble active with flying bugs. Ethan set up my iPod and portable speakers, somewhat impressed that his grandmother had such tech-savvy equipment. I chose the gospel song "God Is Good to Me," sung by the Glide Memorial Choir, a song that I had danced to at my women's retreat when Ken was ill.

We stood atop the hill, in view of the Nebraska State Capitol, each holding our balloons while the words of the song filled the air: "I haven't always been as good as I can be, but God's been good to me." I let my purple balloon go first, saying, "I love you, darling daughter." Standing with our eyes skyward, we four watched my balloon twist around slowly on the wind drifts and then sail high out of sight into the sky. Ethan was next, his light pink balloon easier to see as it traveled more directly upward. We watched till we couldn't see his balloon anymore.

"Who wants to go next?"

Tori grabbed Will's hand and squeezed it. "Let's do it together." And holding hands, they both let their balloons go at the exact same instant, and together we watched them soar.

At dinner that night, at a restaurant with Bill's dad, there was no mention of Corinne or of the day's activities. I was surprised that the children didn't mention what we'd done, as they would normally talk about their day with their dad. Instead, the discussion topic at the table, initiated and continued by Bill's questions, was his father's World War II experiences in the navy. Neither the children nor I had anything to add, nor could we find a bridge to connect with how we had spent our day.

After I had left Nebraska, when the children finally did tell Bill about the ceremony, he got angry because he saw this as my "going around him," which was partly true. On the second anniversary of Corinne's crossing, I followed him out into the backyard so we could talk in private. Standing under the overhang of the house to avoid getting wet from the rain, I apologized for any pain that my actions might have caused him. Corinne's presence felt palatable during our conversation, and as the sun emerged from around the rain clouds, we came to some mutual understanding about our different ways of grieving.

AFTER WORDS

I came to know Steve, a Native American in his mid-thirties, when I directed a social work project in western Nebraska in 1976. The previous fall, my family had buried my kid brother Kenny, and I asked Steve the question most on my mind: "In your culture, when someone close dies, how long does grieving last?" He shook his head, as though he might be too young to know the answer, but he said, "The elders say eight seasons."

Eight seasons—two years. That felt encouraging to me. First off, it meant my sorrow for my brother wouldn't last my whole lifetime and that it was a process that took time. And like the seasons, it was one that could not be hurried.

>>> ▦ <<<

I've come to appreciate that I had a great deal of time with my three adult children, more than I would have had if they'd been healthy and involved in their own lives. With Rose also, our time together in the hospital was a kind of crisis intimacy, of time made more precious because it was fragile and finite. I got to know each of them more fully than would have been likely in different circumstances.

Ever since those intimate moments just before Ken's death, when I felt what seemed like his energy coming inside me, Ken has felt a part of me. I've looked for occasions to do things that he would do, help with causes he cared about. At a conference on HIV/AIDS education for teens, I performed with members of my InterPlay troupe. We danced and sang for the teenagers, who looked askance at first, taking pictures of us old people with their cell phones. I got their rapt attention, however, when I told them my son had died of AIDS. "Heads up, gang! AIDS is not cured. There's medicine, but it has lots of side effects. I know Ken would want you to know how important it is for you to take care of yourselves, to avoid that trip altogether."

I often see things through Ken's eyes, like the movie *Brokeback Mountain,* about two gay cowboys. I'm happy that such a story could be written and made into a film, and I missed being able to see it with Ken. When the movie got an Academy Award, I imagined the over-the-top party Ken would have thrown to celebrate. I shared the joy of two gay men in Iowa planning their upcoming wedding, and I wished Ken could have lived long enough to have one of his own.

People are often amazed when I tell them how well Corinne's children have done. From that first Christmas season after her death, I learned to trust the view that she came to, that she could be mother to her children from wherever she was. That year, Bill had driven the kids to Kansas City to meet Rich and me at an indoor water park. The children burst into the lobby of the hotel, jumping up and down in excitement as they hugged us amid the sparkling lights and tinseled wreaths of the ski lodge setting. Here, in the midst of winter, lay the possibility of a swimming summer: water slides, a gentle stream and floating inner tubes, and spraying shower hoses for spectacular water fights. As the kids toured the children's cabin where they would be staying, I looked over at Bill, who had, by his own choice, celebrated Christmas morning alone with his three children. He managed a faint smile, but he looked terrible, like it had taken nearly every drop of his energy to make it through to where he now stood. I gave him a hug, went into another room, and began praying.

Feeling somewhat desperate, and hoping that the Brazilians are right about people on the other side helping us if we ask, I prayed to Corinne. I thanked her for how well the children are doing: "I know they feel your energy. It's obvious they know they're loved. But honey, you need to send some energy to your husband. This is such a rough time for him. Please help him. Let him feel your love."

And then I watched what to me was a miracle. Gradually, as we got situated in the hotel, got our bathing suits on, and went to the water areas to play, Bill began to revive. By evening, at dinner at his favorite restaurant, he was his old self: joking, telling stories, and enjoying the food and his family.

As it's turned out, Corinne was right about Bill. He is the best dad in the world, and he and the three children have made it by holding on to one another and to the love that Corinne still offers them. I've come to understand that she's not very far away, watching over the kids now as teenagers in a way she would not have been able to do had she stayed on this side.

I believe that one reason my grandchildren have done so well in the years since their mother's death is the way Corinne and Bill included them, in an age-appropriate way, in what was happening during their family ordeal. Corinne's way of describing their system was: "The subjects of illness and death are like the subject of sex. You tell the children what they need to know. You always answer their questions. And you never lie to them." And as the social worker grandmother, I would add, "And you give them the opportunity and support to say good-bye."

Of course I miss my two adult children, often at unexpected times, and I know this will continue throughout my life. One morning, while at the gym taking a Zumba class, I noticed that the woman behind me had brought her adult daughter to exercise with her. My mind returned to the yoga classes Corinne and I took together in Houston, and I thought of a future that will never be. But a few months later, I took twelve-year-old Tori and her best friend with me to a Zumba class I'd found in Nebraska. Since I'd continued dancing, I was able, even at my advanced age, to keep up with those two lively young girls.

I keep Corinne with me by often wearing on a chain around my neck the silver butterfly she gave me for my birthday in Houston. I had it on one day while teaching InterPlay to a group of eight-year-old girls at the Sarah Heinz House in Pittsburgh. They asked about the butterfly, and I used the InterPlay three-sentence story form to tell them:

(1) My daughter gave this butterfly to me for my birthday; (2) She knew that butterflies were special to me; (3) An artist made this from a drawing of a child at the hospital who had cancer.

"Ahh," came a simultaneous, lilting sigh of appreciation from the ten little girls looking up at me, sporting sweet smiles. It surprised me how instinctively these children understood, as indigenous people do, that objects have value related to how they came into being, what they represent, and the gift of love that accompanied them.

>>> ■ <<<

I've told clients, and I know it to be true, that death is not the only way to lose a child, perhaps not even the worst way. After Corinne died, the good and bad news for Kevin was that now instead of being the middle child, where he sometimes could get lost or overlooked, he was the *only child*—and the only one left for me to worry about. During a five-year time frame, I would intermittently lose contact with Kevin. His phone got disconnected, or he moved, or his e-mail wasn't working, or *whatever*. That happened sometimes even before his brother and sister got sick, but it happened more often afterward. Months would go by without word from Kevin and with no way to contact him. Since he was an independent contractor in the LA film industry, there was no employer to call, and since he lived alone with his dogs, there was no roommate to check in with. I would ask him to stay in touch. I would plead for him to leave a message on my voice mail, send me an e-mail. "How will I know when to notify the missing person's bureau?" I would ask. "You know, Kevin, because of my brother's disappearance, and how his body was eventually found, it's hard for me not to worry when I don't hear from you." He would agree in what sounded like an understanding voice, but then things would continue as before.

The only thing that did work was to call his name in a prayer circle at the women's retreat center. It became a joke. "This works better than the phone or computer," I would say to the women. Without fail, the day after I prayed for him out loud in the community, Kevin would call me to check in. I finally decided that this was a confirmation that we were connected in some powerful and unexplainable way and that I would have to, as they say in Alcoholics Anonymous, "Let go and let God."

>>> ▦ <<<

Five years after Corinne's death, Rich and I were planning an Alaskan cruise for our thirtieth wedding anniversary. Doing our separate grief work and being careful to "mind our own business," as they recommend in Al-Anon, had worked well enough for us that we could appreciate what an extraordinary achievement a thirty-year marriage is. We were almost proud of ourselves. And then Rich lost his job.

We'd moved across the country for that job, and when I read that the loss of a job is similar to the loss of a close family member, I asked the universe, "Haven't we lost enough?" At first I feared we might be right back where we were when Corinne died, as a present loss often brings up previous unresolved ones. But the impact this time was very different on each of us. We canceled the cruise and Rich got busy creating a radical redesign of his work life, no small feat during the worst downturn in the economy in our lifetimes. I was able to encourage and support him in both emotional and practical ways, as I had supported my children through their health challenges. Now, having weathered the job-loss storm, we have come to accept that, as Bill and Corinne learned, we will never be able to "cheer one another up" as far as the loss of our children is concerned. We can only turn, separately and together, toward whatever new opportunities life happens to offer us.

People tell me they don't know how I've survived all this, what I've come to know as a "cascade of losses," those trailing rocks and debris that tumble down the hill after the initial boulders have landed. And since my mother did not survive well the loss of her son, I feared I might succumb and follow my own children into death. I do know that much of the time, during my journeys with Ken, with Rose, and even more often with Corinne, I was being held up by a force or energy and led to do the next thing—like writers and composers who report that on some occasions, their stories or melodies come to them fully formed, as if they were taking dictation. Once I was able to get into that place of surrender, to fully accept what I could not change, I was directed and led. My difficulty was, and still is, getting into that place.

The voice I heard when I stepped off the labyrinth in Texas, "*We are the hands of God*," still comes to me. I know this proved to be true for us, as Rich and I; Ken and Kevin; and Bill, Corinne, and the children were sustained by communities of people in Texas and Nebraska during Ken's and Corinne's ordeals and afterward; in California, where I performed the Warrior Dance at a community ritual shortly before Ken was diagnosed; as far away as Australia, where InterPlay participants from all over the world supported Rich and me after Corinne's diagnosis; and later in Pittsburgh, when we relocated there. I've tried to return this favor when I encounter people going through a serious diagnosis or treatment regimen. But I have found in offering help that not everyone is willing to accept it. So I take some credit for our family that we were willing and able to allow people to help us. As Corinne described it, "People want to help, and we help them by allowing them to help us." It's a recognition that we're in this together, and together is how we'll get through it. That's part of how we did, and still do.

>>> ■ <<<

Eight years after Corinne's death, Kevin and I were standing together in a hospital in Palm Springs, California, at the foot of the bed of his partner, Jody. Thankfully, this hospital bed was not like other hospital beds that Kevin and I had stood at together, through the illnesses and deaths of Ken and Corinne. It was unlike the hospital beds that Jody's mother had stood at when Jody had had chemotherapy and radiation for Hodgkin's lymphoma the same year Corinne died.

Kevin and Jody didn't know one another then, and how he found this Cherokee woman, who feels like such a gift to my life, I'm not sure. But there we were, the four of us together, viewing the sonogram of Kevin and Jody's still-developing miracle baby. Jody had been told after her cancer treatments not to expect to be able to conceive a child, and Kevin and our family had long before given up hope that Kevin would become a father. But here we were, teasing each other about the gymnastic, dancelike movements on the screen overhead. The technician called out, "One hundred percent certain, it's a girl!" and she showed us the confirming evidence. As Kevin and I stood with our arms around one another, the squirming little body on the sonogram screen, his baby daughter, my granddaughter, looked right at us and defiantly stuck her thumb in her mouth. Remembering how he had sucked his thumb as a child, Kevin said, "Okay, I can't hold it together any longer." And as his tears of joy and mine began to overflow, we hugged one another.

Five months later came this baby, Kyra Joy. She was three weeks early but timed in such a way as to allow me to fly from Pittsburgh to California, arriving in time to witness the last hour and twenty minutes of her birth.

Stepping into the dimly lit birthing chamber, I felt I was entering an ancient ceremonial space. "The ancestors are all here," I thought, remembering what my midwife friend Jyoti told me when I was with Rose, "The time when life is coming in and the time when life is going out are the times that contain the most light—when the veil between the worlds is lifted."

I felt the energy of the women in our spirituality group who have prayed for one another throughout the past twenty years of our family members' comings in and goings out. I felt the presence of my mother, Jane, the labor and delivery nurse who tried so hard to be present for me when I gave birth to Corinne. Later, my sister would remind me that the birthday of my beloved granddaughter Kyra, whose name means light, was the twenty-ninth anniversary of our mother's crossing and that the day we took Kyra home was the thirteenth anniversary of the day our father died. "Of course the ancestors would be here."

Surrounded by her partner and coach Kevin, the doula, her parents, and a bevy of nurses assisting and providing directions, mother-in-the-making Jody greets me from her bed in the middle of the room: "You made it. I knew you would!" I notice the music and the hypno-birthing tape playing softy in the background. Soon I take my position beside the bed, on the opposite side of her mother, who will become my sister grandmother. Together we stroke and smooth Jody's head to the rhythm of her audible, chant-like breath, accompanying each contraction. In the next hour, with assistance from helpers here and beyond, Jody will demonstrate what it takes to become a warrior mother: the courage to cooperate with her body's messages to relax in the midst of pressure from without and within, the patience to allow her child to move at her own pace, the tremendous strength needed to push and suspend the push, and the wisdom to know what each situation requires.

ACKNOWLEDGMENTS

It takes more than a small village to go from an inspired idea to an actual book. Many people have contributed assistance through the past seven years starting with Marc Nieson, whose invitation to include me in his newly forming writers' group in Pittsburgh enabled me to become a much better writer, as tennis players become better playing with people more skilled than themselves. Under Marc's tutelage, Ken Mohnkern, Holly Maurer-Klein, Margaret Whitford, Ellen Ayoob, Josie Fisher, and later, Michael Grape, and Joann Kielar all influenced me as a writer and a person, and this volume would be very different without their suggestions and encouragement.

I'm grateful for having reconnected with Patricia Lynn Reilly who helped me to develop the mindset and the web platform to carry out such an immense endeavor as a creative non-fiction book. A special appreciation goes to Cynthia Winton-Henry, Glenda Taylor, Victoria Campbell, and Eileen Stukane for their willingness to read and comment on early drafts.

Many thanks to the teachers and fellow students at the Iowa Summer Writing Festival for contributing just what I needed each time I presented myself to their writers' community these past five years; to Cecile Goding for encouragement to write on the subject of illness, to Lon Otto for communicating his enthusiasm for passionate revision, to Ned Stuckey-French for help in building essays from personal stories, to Sarah Saffian for her wise insight into the politics of writing about one's own family, to Carolyn Lieberg for teaching me her practice of focusing on individual words, and to Mary Allen for her exercises to capture the power of Now in spiritual writing.

I owe a debt of deep gratitude to Elizabeth Jarret Andrews, whose skillful guidance a year ago allowed me to re-vision the book's structure, hopefully resulting in a clearer, more readable volume. And to beta readers, Pamela Meadowcroft, Laurel Chaput, and Annie LaGanga, thank you for your kind words of encouragement during times when I was wondering how much longer the journey would be.

As to the actual publishing process – gratitude to Brooke Warner and the She Writes Press team, for seeing to all the technical aspects and for their guidance in educating me about my role in birthing this book and helping it to arrive at a place where it can live on its own.

To my life partner, Richard, who probably should have listened to his family and not gotten involved with me and my children in the first place, I appreciate your willingness to face your own grief and finally read these pages, and to accept so graciously, my interpretation of the events we both shared. To all the friends and family members represented in these pages, whose lives have been deeply intertwined with mine, (those who have crossed and those still here)– I would not, could not, have made it through the events described in these pages without you. May this account of what we went through together be a way of thanking each of you for your contributions and of providing encouragement and strength to those who read these pages as they face similar challenges.

ABOUT THE AUTHOR

photo © Ilana Ransom Toeplitz

S heila K. Collins, PhD has been a dancer, social worker, university professor, clinic director, writer, and improvisational performance artist. She currently directs the Wing & A Prayer Pittsburgh Players, an InterPlay-based improvisational performance troupe that assists human service agencies in serving noble purposes in the Pittsburgh community. Sheila has written about the power of play, dance, and the expressive arts in her book, *Stillpoint: The Dance of Selfcaring, Selfhealing, a playbook for people who do caring work* and on her blog, *Dancing With Everything* which is on her website, sheilakcollins.com.

CPSIA information can be obtained at www.ICGtesting.com
Printed in the USA
LVOW11s0316220316

480208LV00002B/65/P